SEALS AND SEA LIONS

Look for these and other books in the Lucent Endangered Animals and Habitats series:

The Amazon Rain Forest
The Bald Eagle
The Elephant
The Giant Panda
The Oceans
The Rhinoceros
Seals and Sea Lions
The Shark
The Tiger
The Whale
The Wolf

Other related titles in the Lucent Overview series:

Acid Rain
Endangered Species
Energy Alternatives
Garbage
The Greenhouse Effect
Hazardous Waste
Ocean Pollution
Oil Spills
Ozone
Pesticides
Population
Rainforests
Recycling
Vanishing Wetlands
Zoos

Seals and Sea Lions

by Lesley A. DuTemple

Lucent Books, Inc.
San Diego, California

LUCENT Overview Series

Library of Congress Cataloging-in-Publication Data

DuTemple, Lesley A.
Seals & sea lions / by Lesley A. DuTemple.
p. cm. — (Endangered animals & habitats)
Includes bibliographical references (p.) and index.
Summary: Describes the physical characteristics and behavior of seals and sea lions, how they differ from each other, how they relate to humans, how they have become endangered, and what is being done to protect them.
ISBN 1-56006-473-0 (lib. : alk. paper)
1. Pinnipedia—Juvenile literature. Endangered species—Juvenile literature. [1. Seals (Animals) 2. Sea lions. 3. Endangered species.] I. Title. II. Series.
QL737.P6D88 1999
599.79—dc21

98-30303
CIP
AC

P.O. Box 289011, San Diego, CA 92198-9011
Printed in the U.S.A.

Contents

Introduction

FOR CENTURIES, PEOPLE have been fascinated by seals. With their expressive faces and huge eyes, they seem almost human. Some people think they resemble "man's best friend," the dog. But seals also awaken a human fantasy: the ability to inhabit both the sea and the land. Fish inhabit the sea, but not the land. Even whales—mammals with family structures and intelligence similar to our own—can't move between both environments.

Only seals have truly captured the human imagination with their ability to be citizens of both land and sea. History is full of stories about the magical, mysterious powers of seals. One story, the Legend of the Selkie, tells of a mythical seal with the ability to transform into a woman. According to the legend, she and her human husband produced children whose descendants still inhabit Ireland.

Hunted as a natural resource

But fascination with seals has never blinded humans from also seeing seals as a natural resource, something to be exploited. Humans have preyed upon seals since the Stone Age. But in the late eighteenth century and continuing into the 1900s, seal hunters nearly eliminated several species of seals. In their efforts to satisfy a consuming public, sealers killed millions and millions of seals.

Before there was electricity or petroleum products, seals were a useful and needed source of fuel. The blubber from one elephant seal could produce up to eighty gallons of oil. Seal oil was burned in lamps and used as a lubricant. The pelts from seals were used for clothing—at one time, seal-skin coats were the height of fashion throughout Europe and the United States.

But in the quest to obtain more and more seal products, whole populations of seals were nearly wiped out. Hooded, harp, and fur seals were among the victims. Between 1908 and 1910, 4 million northern fur seals were killed on Alaska's Pribilof Islands, their main land habitat. Elephant seals were also severely reduced. Around the world, many seal populations were reduced to only a few individuals.

Killed for their pelts and blubber, seals and sea lions have suffered large population decreases in the nineteenth and twentieth centuries.

But seals are survivors. In the face of seemingly insurmountable odds, some populations have grown again. When populations in one area would drop so low that it was no longer profitable for hunters to go there, those seals were left alone. Gradually, many seal populations were able to increase, but not all—some are still severely endangered and will probably become extinct within the next decade.

Today, seals are no longer hunted for oil but for their fur and other body parts. Many people think all seal hunting should be banned. Others think the public should be educated not to buy seal products, thereby eliminating the market. Many fishermen view seals as a nuisance and kill them whenever they get the chance. To fishermen, seals are very destructive. They eat fish wherever they find them, even if it means destroying a fisherman's net. How seals will survive these threats in the coming decades remains to be seen.

These sea lions play in the waters of Australia. Even where protected, pollution may destroy their habitat.

Endangered by pollution

But hunting by humans is not all that is killing seals—an even greater danger is pollution. In many areas of the globe, seals are dying—even when they are protected and left alone. They are dying because of staggering levels of toxins in their bodies.

In Alaska's Pribilof Islands, seals have been protected for years, yet their population continues to decline. Females are not getting pregnant as often as before, and when they do, the newborn babies are often ill. Seals are barometers for the health of the planet, and many seal populations are doing very poorly. If the oceans have become so polluted that seals can't survive, other sea creatures will be in danger too. The whole chain of life, including humans, is threatened when the oceans are polluted.

The blubber of elephant seals once provided a source of fuel. Elephant seals are now protected and their populations are growing.

The key to questions

Human fascination with seals goes beyond fantasy. It also has a practical side. Like other marine mammals, seals may hold the key to some questions about human survival on the planet. Seals and humans are both mammals, yet seals can virtually live in the water, staying submerged for long periods of time and at great depths. Scientists want to find out how seals have adapted to enable them to accomplish these feats. They want to find out more about seals, not just to "save the seals," but to answer some questions about ourselves.

In the coming years, perhaps we can strike a balance between seals and humans. Although we inhabit a different environment than seals, both environments exist together on a single planet.

1

The Basics About Seals

SEALS ARE ONE of the most interesting animals known to humans. On land, they can be mistaken for a rock or a pile of seaweed—or even a dog. But in water, they are so fast and graceful, they look like birds zooming beneath the waves. And when they poke their heads curiously above the water, they resemble a bobbing piece of driftwood. But seals are not dogs, birds, rocks, or pieces of seaweed. Seals are mammals—mammals so unique, they occupy a class by themselves.

Seals are pinnipeds

The word "seal," as commonly used, actually refers to three different families—all of them belong to the order of mammals called "pinnipeds," meaning "fin-footed." The three families are: seals, sea lions and fur seals, and walruses. All pinnipeds have four flippers.

Pinnipeds have been on earth for millions of years. The oldest known pinniped is called Enaliarctos. Enaliarctos lived about 22.5 million years ago. Although fossil bits and pieces were found in the past century, a complete fossil skeleton of Enaliarctos was not found until 1989.

By carefully studying its fossil bones, scientists have been able to reconstruct what Enaliarctos looked like. Bones do more than just indicate the general size and shape of an animal. In addition to providing support for the animal, its skeleton also provides attachment points for muscles. If the attachment point on a skeleton is large, scientists know that a large muscle connected at that place. In this way, scientists can reconstruct the true shape of Enaliarctos because they know where the large and small muscle groups were.

Scientists know that Enaliarctos used all four limbs, as well as large muscles along its spine, for swimming. In addition to being a powerful swimmer, Enaliarctos was probably a good walker. As author Dorothy Hinshaw Patent points out, "Enaliarctos could turn its hind flippers forward for walking on land. . . . Its hindlimb bones have large attachment points for certain muscles, indicating that it probably was more active on land than the pinnipeds of today."[1]

Those Amazing Pinnipeds

Smallest Pinniped: Baikal seal, a freshwater seal that lives only in Lake Baikal in south-central Russia. They're usually less than 4 feet (1.25 m) long and weigh about 72 pounds (32 kg). Arctic ringed seals are the smallest "ocean" seals.

Largest Pinniped: Male southern elephant seals. They can reach lengths of nearly 20 feet (5 m) and weigh more than 8,000 pounds (4,000 kg). Southern elephant seals are found around Antarctica and the southern Pacific.

Fastest Swimmer: California sea lions can swim 25 miles per hour (40 kph). They are found on the Pacific coast, ranging from California to Baja California.

Fastest Runner: Crabeater seals can run nearly 16 miles per hour (25 kph) across the ice. They live in Antarctica.

Deepest Diver: Northern elephant seals can dive more than 4,000 feet (1,220 m) deep. They range from the Farallon Islands, off the coast of northern California, to the Baja peninsula of Mexico.

Longest Time Underwater: Weddell seals stay underwater for more than an hour. They live in Antarctica.

Longest Living: A ringed seal that lived to be forty-six years old holds the pinniped longevity record. Ringed seals live in the Arctic.

Scientists used to think that sea lions, fur seals, and walruses were descended from a bearlike creature, whereas seals were descended from a doglike creature. But a comparison of DNA from Enaliarctos's skeleton with DNA from present-day pinnipeds shows that all three families (seals, fur seals and sea lions, and walruses) share common traits. This indicates that all pinnipeds probably descended from the same ancestor.

Differences between pinnipeds

Though most pinnipeds look fairly alike, there are several distinct differences between the three families. Their scientific names are in Latin. Phocidae is all true seals. Otariidae is sea lions and fur seals. Odobenidae is the walrus. There are seventeen species of true seals, thirteen species of sea lions and fur seals, and only one species of walrus.

Easily identified by their giant bodies and large tusks, walruses are perhaps the most recognizable of the pinnipeds.

Most people can recognize a walrus. They are the only pinnipeds with huge canine tusks. In addition to giant tusks, walruses often have giant bodies: The name "walrus" comes from a Norwegian word meaning "whale horse."

The other two families of pinnipeds, "true seals" and "sea lions and fur seals," are also easily distinguished. Scientists also refer to these two families as "earless seals" (true seals) and "eared seals" (sea lions and fur seals). Except for the walrus, any pinniped could be called a "seal." It's just a question of what kind of seal it is: true or eared.

Eared seals like this one can be identified by the small visible ear lobes on the sides of their heads.

True seals have no external ear flaps, only tiny openings on the sides of their heads that lead directly to the internal ear. Sea lions and fur seals have small visible ear lobes, hence the name "eared seals." The head of a true seal is rounded and has no discernible neck. Eared seals have pointed, narrower heads and a longer neck.

There are other ways to distinguish a true seal from an eared seal. When true seals are on land, they pull themselves forward with their front flippers, using the strong muscles in their back to hunch along like a giant caterpillar. Meanwhile, their back flippers lie flat and drag behind. Eared seals, however, tuck their hind flippers underneath themselves and actually walk around using all four flippers like short, squat legs. Some even manage a lopsided run.

In water, true seals can also be distinguished from sea lions and fur seals. True seals use their hind flippers and rear body to propel themselves through the water. They swing their bodies side-to-side with a powerful swishing motion. They use their front flippers only for steering and balance.

Eared seals propel themselves through the water with their front flippers, using them like giant oars. Their hind flippers are primarily used for steering and balance. Eared seals, particularly sea lions, are the speed rockets of the pinniped family. When swimming, they can easily reach speeds of twenty-five miles per hour.

The largest and smallest ocean-dwelling pinnipeds in the world are both true seals. The smallest that is commonly found, the ringed seal, lives in the Arctic and North Atlantic Oceans. It usually weighs under 250 pounds and measures less than six feet long. (The Baikal seal is actually smaller than a ringed seal but lives only in the freshwater Lake Baikal in southern Russia.) The largest pinniped is the southern elephant seal of the Antarctic Ocean. Males can weigh more than eight thousand pounds and measure twenty feet long. The weight and length of all other pinnipeds, including walruses, fall somewhere between these two extremes.

Gathering in rookeries

Although pinnipeds spend much of their time in the water, all of them go ashore to mate and have their young. Like other mammals, pinnipeds give birth to live young who nurse. Every year, large numbers of the same species gather together to mate, give birth, and raise their young. For reasons unknown, they usually gather in the exact same spot, year after year.

The areas where pinnipeds gather are called rookeries. Small islands with no predators are favorite rookery sites. Isolated beaches and ice floes are also places where pinnipeds gather.

When large numbers of the same species gather together in one place, it is easier for the males and females to find each other and ensures a more successful mating. But the tendency to gather together in rookeries has also contributed to the death of millions of seals. When the seals are concentrated in one place, it is easy for human hunters to kill them in huge numbers, in a short period of time with little effort.

Cows and pups

Pinniped babies are called pups. Female pinnipeds, called cows, usually give birth to only one pup each year. Unlike other mammals, pinnipeds are born with their eyes open and can move around almost immediately after birth. The flippers of a newborn pinniped pup are strong and

Although seals have more success with mating when they gather in large numbers in rookeries, they are also more vulnerable to hunters in this setting. Here, thousands of seals gather at Cape Cross, Namibia.

sturdy, unlike the legs of many other newborn mammals. Pups can flap around right away, and some, like the harbor seal, can even swim. Most pups, though, stay firmly ashore for the first several weeks of their lives.

Like all other newborn mammals, pups nurse. Pinniped milk is thick, oily, and rich with nutrients. Pups grow quickly, and the rich milk helps them build up an insulating supply of blubber, or body fat.

Cows usually stay continuously with their pups for only a short time. Some species leave their pups a few hours after birth to briefly hunt and eat. Other species leave their pups after a few days, sometimes staying absent from the rookery for as long as a week. Even the most attentive cows will stay with their pup for only about a week before they start leaving for extended periods of time to hunt for food. As the late ocean explorer Jacques Cousteau noted, "A good part of a sea lion's time is spent in the water. Sea lion mothers sometimes remain in the sea for several days before returning to land to nurse their young."[2]

With thousands of pinnipeds in a rookery, and all of them moving about, it seems impossible for a returning mother to locate her baby among them. Yet seal cows are able to find their pups when they come ashore, no matter how long they've been apart.

Pinniped pups like these are left alone in rookeries for long periods of time early in their lives and stay ashore for several weeks after birth.

At birth, both cow and pup sniff each other carefully and make special identifying sounds. This brief period of imprinting and bonding enables both of them to nearly always find each other among the thousands of other pinnipeds in the rookery. Cows, in particular, recognize their own pup very clearly. If a pup other than her own approaches, the cow will push it aside, sometimes severely injuring it. The pups don't seem to recognize their mother as easily as she recognizes them—they'll usually swarm any cow that comes ashore, hoping to be able to nurse.

Dangers in the rookery

Rookeries have the atmosphere of a circus, with cows calling out to their pups and pups calling for their mothers. Thousands of pinnipeds roam about barking, calling, and squabbling with each other. Even without the threat of human hunters, life in a rookery can be dangerous for a pup. In addition to often going days without food, pups have to avoid the very real danger of getting injured or killed. Male pinnipeds, called bulls, crash about the rookery, bellowing and fighting with other bulls as they attempt to mate with the cows. Some gather together large harems, or groups of cows. Others roam about, mating with any cow they can claim.

Bulls come to the rookeries only to mate; they have nothing to do with caring for the pups. Bulls are able to breed when they're about six years old. In many species, the bulls establish territories within the rookery and fight any bulls that invade their space, particularly those with established harems. A pup that gets in the way of these battles can easily be trampled to death.

Cows are able to mate when they're two to four years old. Cows are also able to mate again only a few weeks after giving birth, so pups may also be trampled by bulls trying to mate with their mothers.

In observing sea lion pups, Jacques Cousteau noted,

> They have a difficult life in the midst of the constant agitation of the harem of adults. They are born with their eyes open, and they are already furred at birth. They nurse at irregular

Training Sea Lions

People watching sea lions perform at marine parks often wonder just how these amazing animals are trained. As most trainers point out, they're not really "training" the seal to do new behavior; instead, they're using behaviors the animal does naturally, then getting the seal to associate the natural behavior with a signal and a reward. By combining a series of natural behaviors with commands and rewards, trainers are able to "create" a trained seal.

The U.S. Navy has been working with marine mammals since 1960. Seals learn very quickly. When their quick learning ability is combined with their amazing water abilities, seals perform tasks that humans only dream of. They also seem to like humans, which makes it easy for trainers to work with them.

One of the navy's projects employs sea lions to locate and attach recovery devices to test items that have been fired or dropped into the ocean. Recovery tasks can be dangerous for humans but sea lions perform the same tasks quickly and easily. The device to be recovered emits a sound that the seal can hear. It then swims to the object, holding a long recovery rope in its mouth. The seal attaches the rope to the object and returns to the surface for a reward of fish. Once the rope is attached, navy personnel can haul the object to the surface.

By working with marine mammals, the navy hopes to learn more about their abilities, and give human divers some needed help.

intervals and they take several liters of milk at a single nursing. Between nursing sessions, they teach themselves to swim, first in the pools of water left by the tide, then, later, in the sea.[3]

Other dangers lurk at the edge of a rookery. In the Antarctic, leopard seals prowl the waters around rookeries, hoping to catch any unwary pups that venture into the water for swimming lessons. In the Arctic, cows build sheltering snow caves for themselves and their pup, right on the ice floes. Polar bears roam freely over the ice floes, smelling out the caves and stomping and crashing down the roofs to break in and get the pups.

Pups on their own

Some cows allow their pups to go out on their own in as little as seven weeks, while other pinniped species keep their pups around for a couple of years. After about four months, though, many species of pups are entirely on their own.

In general, mammals mature slower than other animals. For many mammal babies, being on their own after only four months would mean certain death. But pinnipeds seem to mature faster than other mammals. At four months of age, nearly all seals can swim, hunt and catch fish, and get around quite well.

Once the seals are on their own in the wild, scientists are not sure how long they live. Some research shows that cows should naturally live about twenty years and bulls about fourteen years. But scientists don't really know because it's

Pinniped pups usually spend four months with their mothers. After this time the pups have developed the skills needed to survive on their own.

hard to track seals in the wild. In captivity, though, pinnipeds live to be about twenty years old. Since captive pinnipeds receive excellent care and plenty of food, those in the wild probably don't live quite that long.

Where pinnipeds live

Pinnipeds are found all over the world, from the polar ice caps to the equator. But the three different families tend to congregate in different areas of the globe.

Most true seals live in the colder waters, especially around the polar regions of the globe—the exception being two species of monk seals. Hawaiian monk seals live in the warm Pacific waters of the Hawaiian Islands. Mediterranean monk seals live in and around the Mediterranean Sea. Both species are extremely endangered—monk seals have been on the worldwide "Top Ten" endangered list for years. A third species of monk seal, the Caribbean monk seal, is already extinct. All monk seals are unique in being the only pinnipeds to live in tropical waters.

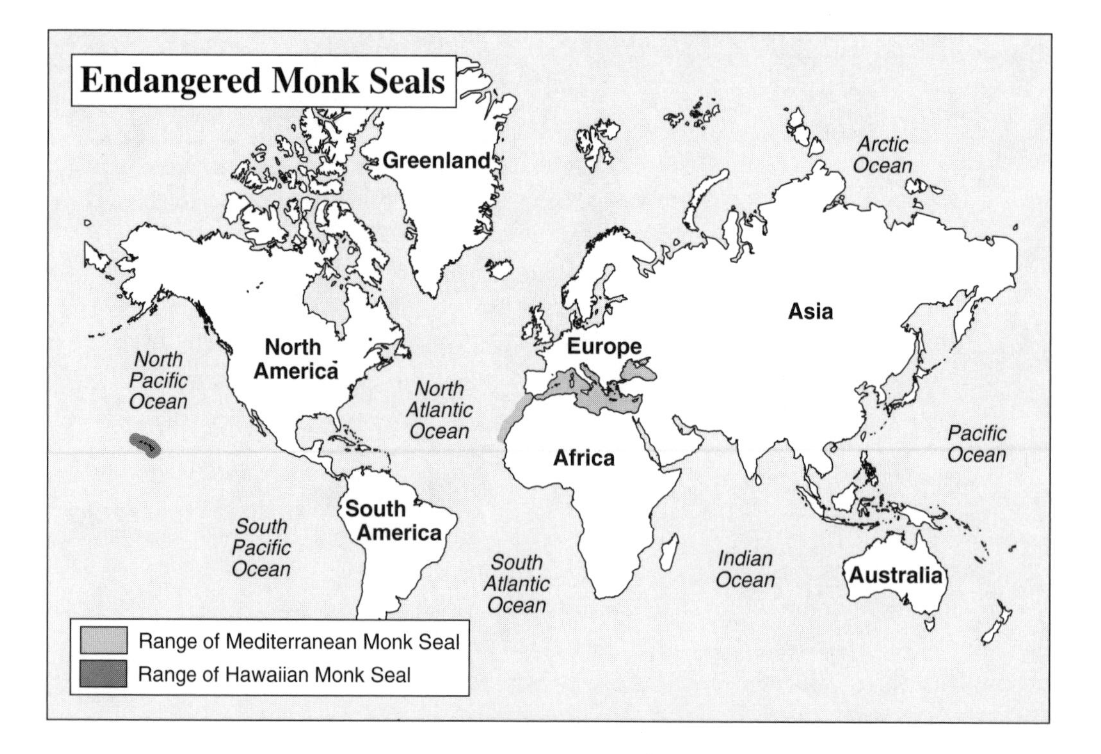

Eared seals usually inhabit the more temperate seas of the globe, including the oceans around Australia, New Zealand, and South America. The California sea lion is found off the coast of California and Mexico. The northern fur seal is the only eared seal to inhabit Arctic waters, and southern fur seals can be found in Antarctica. But most sea lions and fur seals live from the edges of the polar regions to the middle range of the globe.

A perfectly adapted body

Pinnipeds live on land. But they spend so much time in the water, you could say they also live in the water. Their bodies are actually better adapted to living in water than on land. They can even sleep in water. According to author John Bonnett Wexo, "In shallow water, they may sink to the bottom and sleep while holding their breath. They rise to the surface from time to time to get some air, then sink again. In deeper water, they may float upright with just the tip of their noses above water."[4]

Most pinnipeds inhabit cold waters, even those that live off the coasts of California, Mexico, and Australia. Water pulls body heat away much faster than air does—as much as twenty-three times faster. As mammals, pinnipeds maintain a constant body temperature, no matter how cold the water is. To keep up their temperature while spending hours in cold water, pinnipeds have developed special adaptations.

A thick layer of blubber, or body fat, just under their skin acts as insulation. Pinnipeds develop blubber almost at birth. After a few weeks of nursing, even young pups develop a good layer of blubber. Besides helping to prevent heat loss, blubber also stores food energy. Blubber helps pups survive when their mothers are at sea. And blubber helps mature seals survive when food is in short supply.

Fur is also a good insulator. But fur slows down seagoing mammals when they swim, by creating drag. Although all pinnipeds have fur, the ones that spend the most time in the water, like elephant seals, have the shortest fur. Only the northern fur seal has a thick furry coat.

Valves that regulate a pinniped's blood circulation help keep it warm in cold water and cool in the hot sun.

All the adaptations that pinnipeds have for staying warm in frigid waters can cause problems when they're on land. Any kind of physical activity on land can cause a pinniped's body to overheat. To avoid overheating, pinnipeds have special valves that regulate their blood circulation. When pinnipeds are in water, their circulation directs the flow of blood away from their blubber and outer skin, so less heat loss occurs through contact with the water. But when on land, their circulation directs the flow of blood through the blubber and outer skin, so more heat loss occurs and the pinniped can cool off. When pinnipeds get too warm, the circulation to the bare parts of their bodies—their flippers—increases. On hot days, eared seals are often seen waving their flippers about in the air, cooling off.

More adaptations

Pinnipeds spend a lot of time in the water because that's where the food is. In order to feed successfully, they need to stay underwater for long periods of time.

Although they have to breathe air to survive, pinnipeds dive long and deep when hunting for food. They usually stay underwater for only a few minutes, or perhaps fifteen minutes, but a few species can easily stay submerged for more than one hour. And most species can dive to a depth of two thousand feet. Without mechanical aids, humans can rarely stay underwater for more than three minutes or go deeper than twenty feet. How do pinnipeds do it?

When pinnipeds start to dive, the air in their lungs converts into their bloodstream. Pinnipeds have greater blood volume than other mammals and also more hemoglobin, which holds oxygen in their bloodstream. As pinnipeds continue to dive deeper, they use oxygen from the hemoglobin. They don't have to rely on holding their breath, as humans do.

The muscles of pinnipeds are also specially adapted to hold oxygen. Pinniped muscles have more myoglobin than

Pinnipeds are able to dive deep for long periods of time in search of food. Here, a sea lion dives among the coral reefs near Australia.

other mammals. Just as hemoglobin stores oxygen in the bloodstream, myoglobin stores oxygen in the muscles. When pinnipeds are underwater, they're still receiving oxygen through the myoglobin cells.

Although pinnipeds are more active in the water than on land, in water their bodies actually use less oxygen than when they're on land. When they dive, their blood circulates mostly to their brain. Other body organs, like the liver and kidneys, reduce their oxygen use. Even their heart slows down, sometimes to one-tenth of its normal rate.

Hunters of the ocean

Pinnipeds are predators and carnivores. They hunt and feed on various kinds of fish, seabirds, squid, and krill. Walruses, leopard seals, and sea lions are also known to feed on the pups of other pinniped species. On one island in Alaska, Steller's sea lions are responsible for eating 6 percent of the northern fur seal pups every year. In general, pinnipeds are opportunistic feeders—they'll eat whatever they can, whenever the opportunity arises.

Because pinnipeds primarily eat fish, they are often in conflict with the fishing industry. Seals eat a lot of fish. One seal can eat approximately seven pounds of fish every day. In the ocean, seals tend to congregate in large groups near large schools of fish. The seals are just staying close to their food supply. But fishermen also seek out large schools of fish. As more fish are caught by humans, the seals get more aggressive about obtaining fish for themselves. When fishermen get only small catches, they blame the seals for eating so much fish. But other people don't think it's the seals' fault. They think that fish catches are low because of overfishing and disease from pollution.

Natural predators and dangers

Seals are predators, but they are also prey. As Jacques Cousteau has pointed out, "They have enemies in addition to man: sharks, and especially killer whales."[5]

Throughout the oceans of the world, orcas ("killer whales") prey upon pinnipeds. In South America, particu-

Pinnipeds are prey to various large sea animals such as orca whales. Here, an orca hunts sea lions off the Argentinian shore in South America.

larly in Patagonia, orcas actually swim onto beaches to capture seals. Sharks also prey upon pinnipeds. And in the Antarctic, leopard seals are ferocious predators of smaller pinniped species. Within any rookery many pinnipeds will have large scars, often the result of encounters with orcas, sharks, or leopard seals.

In the Arctic, ringed seals are the favorite food of polar bears. A polar bear will stand for hours at a breathing hole in the ice, just waiting for a seal to surface for a breath of air. Then with a swift strike of its massive and sharply clawed paw, the polar bear swats the seal out of the water.

Pinnipeds face other natural dangers. Storms are very hard on pups and young pinnipeds. When El Niño created storms along the Pacific coast in the winter of 1997–98, marine wildlife rescue centers were filled beyond capacity with sick, exhausted young sea lions. Most were just too small and young to withstand the drenching rains and buffeting winds of the continuous storms. As people found them on the beaches of California, they would call, or bring them into, marine centers. Without human help, many would have died. As it was, by February 1998 most rescue centers were unable to accept any more pinnipeds—they had no space left.

Endangered pinnipeds?

Although seals were hunted almost to extinction in recent centuries, today many species have rebounded. Some populations even number in the millions, although several species remain on the brink of extinction. Seals are still hunted for their fur and other body parts, but they are no longer hunted primarily for their oil. The discovery of petroleum probably saved most species of whales and pinnipeds from extinction.

But many pinnipeds still face problems. As the human population expands, so does the demand for natural resources such as land and fish. Pollution of those resources also rises. Many seal populations suffer as a result of this encroachment on their habitat. In the coming years, humans will need to find ways to share resources if pinniped populations are to survive.

2

Hunting Seals

HUMANS HAVE HUNTED seals for hundreds of years. Along with walruses, polar bears, whales, and caribou, native peoples of the far north depended on seals for their very survival. In the frozen lands of the north, seals were a genuine crop. There were no grocery stores, no fruit trees, no gardens. Seals were harvested, and every single part was used. The fur was used for clothing, the meat for food, the blubber for both oil and food, the skins for kayaks, shoes, and shelters. Even the bones and teeth were carved into decorative objects or used for tools. Each year, the bladders were thrown back into the ocean during a ceremony honoring Sedna, the seal goddess of the Eskimo peoples. Even today, Eskimo peoples continue the tradition, and honor Sedna with a festival each fall.

Although seals were hunted extensively by northern Native American peoples, the seal populations there never experienced any significant decline. According to the late ocean explorer Jacques Cousteau, "Eskimos are content to kill only that number of animals which is necessary to their own survival."[6]

Even today, this practice still holds true among modern Eskimos. "Subsistence hunters throughout the Arctic kill more than 100,000 ringed seals annually," says researcher Stephen Leatherwood.[7] Although that may sound like a lot, it's a small amount compared to the total seal population.

The Legend of Sedna

In countries where seals are abundant, many legends exist about the origins of seals. From the Arctic, this Eskimo legend tells how the first seal came to be. It appears in *The Sea World Book of Seals and Sea Lions* by Phyllis Roberts Evans.

> There once was a beautiful Eskimo girl named Sedna who unfortunately fell in love with a wizard. Such a thing was absolutely forbidden because the wizard was magic, supposedly very evil, and had the ability to cast spells. Sedna's father was so angry with her that he did a dreadful thing. He cut off her hands and legs and tossed her into the sea. He expected that she would drown, and never again disgrace him.
>
> When the wizard discovered that Sedna had been thrown into the sea, he became very upset. He turned himself into a seagull and flew over the water looking for her. He didn't want her to die, so when he finally found her, he changed her into an animal that could live in the water. That creature was a seal—a beautiful, graceful animal without hands or legs. She became the goddess of the underworld, someone to be honored for all time. She was said to control the animals of the sea, and the legend went that if the Eskimos did not please her, she would drive the seals, whales, and other sea creatures away.

Commercial sealing

In the mid-1800s, though, many things changed. Whaling was already a large industry, and when it was discovered that seal blubber could also be rendered into oil to burn in lamps, seal hunting became a huge global industry. At this time when there was no electricity or petroleum, seals were considered a natural resource—just as underground oil is considered a natural resource today. Seals were big enough to be worth killing, yet small enough not to fight back. And seals provided an extra benefit that whales did not: fur pelts. In addition to their blubber, seals had thick, luxurious fur that could be made into clothing.

Although Eskimos considered seals a natural resource, they never exploited the populations to the extent that Europeans, Canadians, Americans, and other non-native peoples did. Most Eskimos used kayaks and harpoons to hunt seals, which gave the seals at least a fighting chance of survival.

An Eskimo sits, his hunting gear ready, waiting to catch a seal. Although Eskimos never exploited seals, they viewed them as a valuable natural resource.

But in the second half of the nineteenth century, hunting methods changed dramatically. Guns and explosives became more widely used all over the globe. And for seals, this spelled trouble. Instead of kayaks and harpoons, the seals were hunted from huge ships with guns and explosives. The seals' habit of gathering together in rookeries made it all the easier for hunters to kill them. The Canadian Sealers Association reports that "the first recorded commercial seal harvest was likely as early as 1874," although commercial harvests in other parts of the world were occurring in the late 1700s.[8] Throughout the late nineteenth and early twentieth centuries, hundreds of thousands of seals were slaughtered each year. In only a three-year period, from 1908 to 1910, 4 million seals were killed on the Pribilof Islands alone.

By any standards, the seal deaths were cruel. Many of them were shot, clubbed, speared, or skinned alive. Often only the pelt was taken and the seal's body was left. Other times the seal was attacked and left to die.

Declining seal populations

As seal population numbers plummeted, seals became harder to find. So sealers started traveling farther, hoping to find new populations. Any time they found a new seal population, or colony, those seals were also killed. Almost systematically, seal populations were nearly wiped out around the globe, some of them never to fully recover. In 1792, the Juan Fernández fur seal population off the coast of South America numbered over 3 million. By 1807 less than 300 remained.

"The story is the same as the story of whaling," says author Vassili Papastavrou. "The sealers took so many animals that there were almost none left."[9]

Seal products

Seal blubber was originally rendered down for use in oil lamps. Later, other uses were found. Seal blubber was used in lipstick, soaps, margarines, and lubricants. The meat was canned and used as pet food. Walruses were

Seal populations were wiped out in the late nineteenth century as a result of an increase in a wide range of seal products used by humans.

killed for their ivory, and Steller's sea lions were killed for their long whiskers, which were used as pipe cleaners.

In the late 1800s, a way was found to remove the stiff outer guard hairs on a seal's pelt, leaving the soft underfur. This discovery further ensured the demise of seals, as clothing made from seal fur became wildly popular throughout the United States and Europe during the late nineteenth and early twentieth centuries. Huge colonies were wiped out in only a few years as the demand for seal pelts soared.

Seals come back

When the seal population in an area declined drastically enough, sealers left them alone—not for environmental or ethical reasons, but because it was no longer profitable. To make a sealing venture worthwhile, sealers had to return with a lot of pelts. If most of the seals in a particular area had already been slaughtered, sealers didn't bother to go there anymore. Killing seals might have been easy, but getting to them was anything but easy. Most seals inhabit frigid polar waters, difficult areas for hunters to travel in any time of the year. To undertake polar travel, the "catch" had to be worthwhile. It simply became unprofitable to go so far, for so little return.

During this period of decline, in the early 1900s, seals showed how resilient most populations are. Once they were left alone—with only a few seals in rookeries that had once held millions—most populations started to rebound. But this resiliency on the part of seals has been a double-edged sword. According to modern-day sealers, the very fact that seals have come back from such low numbers indicates that they reproduce rapidly and need to be "culled," or hunted. "If you do not remove approximately 150,000 seal pups from their birthplace every year, the population of seals will get out of control," quote researchers Janet Herrlinger and Peter Erdman in their research draft.[10]

The decline and rise of sealing

In the first half of the twentieth century, professional sealing declined. Like whaling, the industry almost vanished with the discovery of underground oil and all the uses of related petroleum products. Sealing on a large scale just was not profitable, at least for Europeans and Americans. Eskimos and other native peoples still continued sealing, as they had always done. It was during this time that seal populations were able to make their biggest recoveries.

But then in the 1950s, sealing became profitable again. The Norwegians invented large steel ships capable of breaking through ice without sustaining damage. This, combined with a surge in demand for seal pelt clothing, sent a new generation of sealers into areas that had not been previously exploited.

The year 1952 was a landmark in the sealing industry. It was the first year in the centuries-old history of sealing when it became more profitable to hunt seals for their pelts than for their blubber. Seal blubber was no longer needed for oil after the discovery of petroleum. Now pelts were the most valuable part of a seal. The reason? The popularity of the clothing made from the white fur of the harp seal pup, or "whitecoat." But the hunt for whitecoats also set off a reaction of vast and far-reaching public opposition to the practice of sealing.

The peak hunting year for whitecoats was 1964. In addition to men and ships, 150 airplanes and helicopters took part in the hunt. Many inexperienced sealers were sent on the ice, and they often maimed and wounded seals, leaving them to die. Hundreds of thousands of seal pups were clubbed to

Exposing the Trinket Trade

In the 1970s, when the public first voiced concern over the seal hunt, the Canadian government insisted that the commercial seal hunt was necessary because it brought in large amounts of money. The environmental group Greenpeace was suspicious and conducted their own research. A Greenpeace fact sheet entitled "Harp Seals: Fragile Victory" reports the following:

> Market research was begun in the late 1970s to determine what was produced from the seal pelts and who was profiting from the hunt. The results were jarring. Ninety percent of the seal pelts taken by Canada and Norway were exported to western European countries, transformed into trifles such as fur-covered trinkets, fur-trimmed gloves, and après-ski boots. The carcasses were left to rot on the ice with only a small percentage of the meat being consumed. The lion's share of the profits from both the Canadian and Norwegian hunts went to a large Norwegian corporation, G.C. Rieber & Co. of Bergen.
>
> This information totally contradicted the Canadian government's defense of the sealing industry for its vital contribution to the economy of eastern Canada.
>
> In actuality, even a relatively profitable year (such as 1978) generated only a little over $6 million in revenue. This figure is offset by the cost of federal government administration, scientific and enforcement personnel, Coast Guard personnel, icebreakers, and aircraft ($.5 to 1.5 million annually); losses to the Canadian economy from boycotts against Canadian tourism, goods and services due to the hunt (at least $1 million annually); and the costs of defending the seal hunt against protest groups ($1 to 2 million annually).

death; many others were skinned alive. Afterward, scientists estimated that over the years, the population had been reduced by nearly half its original numbers. Clearly, something would have to be done.

A public outcry

Regulations proposed by scientists might have helped, but ultimately, cameras proved to be far more effective in curtailing the hunt for whitecoats. With their huge dark eyes and fluffy white coats, baby harp seals are incredibly photogenic—as is their blood on snow. In the 1970s, observers from various environmental organizations, such as Greenpeace and the World Wildlife Fund, started photographing the whitecoat hunt and publishing the images around the globe. The public outcry was instantaneous and overwhelmingly unanimous: seal hunting was inhumane, and sealers were barbarians.

Almost overnight, sealers found themselves pitted against the public and environmental groups, fighting for their livelihood, and in many instances, their culture and way of life. Nowadays, many sealers are Newfoundlanders and other Arctic peoples, often of Eskimo or Inuit descent. They hunt seals for many reasons—because their ancestors always did, and because they use seal parts to feed and clothe their own families. But they also hunt seals to sell to other people. There are very few ways for native peoples living in the northeastern Canadian provinces to earn money. Selling the seals they hunt provides the cash that helps them survive and keep living on the land of their ancestors.

As researchers Janet Herrlinger and Peter Erdman note, "A Newfoundland fisherman used to estimate that if he worked hard, he would earn only a couple of thousand dollars during the four to six weeks of the seal pup hunt. Nevertheless, in many cases this made up almost a third of his yearly income."[11]

Within most Arctic communities, seals are not just a natural resource; they are vital to the community's way of life and a critical source of cash for the whole community. Seal

"THERE WE WERE, ALMOST ALONE ON THE ICE, FACING TWENTY-FIVE POUNDS OF FEROCIOUS BABY SEAL, WITH ONLY OUR CLUBS FOR PROTECTION!"

hunting is integral to the entire economy of the native peoples of the Arctic. Most sealers are baffled and angry over the outcry against sealing. For many of them, seals are part of their daily lives. They feel they know and understand the seal herds far better than any environmental organization does.

Within Arctic fishing communities, such as those in Newfoundland and other parts of northern Canada, seals are also viewed as competitors. Arctic fishermen claim that one adult harp seal can eat more than seven pounds of fish every day, for a total of 1.25 tons every year. If a rookery

On the Ice—"Protecting" Seals

Public attention was first drawn to the commercial seal hunt in the mid-1960s. Ironically, it was the Canadian government itself that caused the outcry. In making a government film to promote tourism in Quebec, they filmed a sequence meant to portray the ancient struggle between man and nature. The sequence showed newborn harp seals being beaten to death with spiked clubs. When the film aired, the public and conservation groups alike were horrified.

Conservation groups went into action. A fact sheet issued by Greenpeace entitled "Harp Seals: Fragile Victory" tells what its workers were willing to go through to get the seal hunt stopped.

> In 1976 we sent a team to the scene of the slaughter. Our purpose was two-fold: to physically save seals by shielding them with our bodies, and to bring the kill to the attention of the world. We believed the public would not condone the largest slaughter of nursing wild mammals on earth. We were right. The actions of Greenpeace and other environmental groups sparked unprecedented international concern over a wildlife issue.
>
> From 1976 to 1985, Greenpeace sent expeditions to Canada. We boarded the ships to prevent their departure from port, covered the pups with harmless green dye to make their coats worthless to the fur trade, and shielded pups from sealers' clubs. Protesters were arrested on board the *Rainbow Warrior* in 1981 and 1982 by Canadian fisheries officials. In response to Greenpeace actions, the government quickly passed addenda to the ill-named "Seal Protection Regulations," which made it illegal for all but sealers to approach a seal. As a result, Greenpeace activists were arrested every year (except 1980) for violating the "Seal Protection Regulations."

Greenpeace was not the only environmental group to employ such drastic measures. Many other conservation groups, including the International Fund for Animal Welfare, used the same tactics, turning Canada's annual seal hunt into a true media event.

During the 1970s and 1980s, organizations such as Greenpeace and the International Fund for Animal Welfare publicly protested the hunting of seals.

An Inuit hunter drags his catch back home. Some native tribes in the Arctic still hunt seals for food and other necessities.

of 1 million seals lives near an Arctic fishing village, this kind of depletion could have a serious effect on the whole economy.

Commercial seal hunting banned

As the images of bloody baby seals flashed around the world, the market for seal fur clothing dwindled. In 1988, the Canadian government officially banned commercial seal hunting. The government quotas continued to allow native peoples to hunt and kill one hundred thousand seals a year—some of them whitecoats—but there was, and is currently, very little market demand for seal fur products.

Because of this change in public attitudes, many Newfoundland villages had unemployment rates of more than 80 percent in the early 1990s. Sealing was their way of life and a critical source of cash that allowed them to stay on ancestral land. Modern technology has made it possible for

Arctic peoples to obtain other food and not rely solely upon seals for their survival. Although most of the hunted seals are now sold to outsiders, seal hunting remains an integral part of their culture. But, for peoples of the Arctic, a culture thousands of years old is in danger of vanishing forever—and they are angry. They point out that it was not northern native peoples who overexploited the seal, yet they are left paying the price for the actions of Europeans, Canadians, and Americans.

3

Fighting for Fish

AS LONG AS seals have been on earth, they have eaten fish. And as long as humans have been on earth, they too have eaten fish. For thousands of years, humans and seals—and the fish they eat—coexisted peacefully. But problems are developing. Being hunted for their pelts, blubber, and oil is not the only threat seals face when it comes to humans. Recently, seals have been viewed as competitors for the fish in the ocean. Fish populations have declined, so there are not as many fish in the oceans as there used to be. Some people think seals are to blame, for eating too many fish. Other people think that overfishing by humans is the problem.

Seals, fish, and Eskimos

Eskimo and Inuit peoples have had the longest-running, and the closest, relationship with seals. But Eskimo and Inuit cultures rely on more than just seals; they coexist with, and utilize, all creatures in the northern landscapes and oceans—especially fish. Northern native peoples have always relied on both seals and fish—particularly salmon and cod—for their survival.

Historically, northern native peoples have had a balanced relationship with their environment. Although seals eat fish, Eskimos and Inuits never thought of seals as "competitors" for the fish in the ocean. The fact that seals eat fish has always been a normal part of life in the frozen north. It didn't mean there would not be enough fish for

Although Eskimos killed seals for food and their pelts, they did not hunt them in mass numbers. Here, Eskimo women carry a dead seal back to camp.

the Eskimos. There was always enough. For many centuries, Eskimos, seals, and fish coexisted in the frozen north, jointly sharing the resources.

According to Eric S. Grace, "Native peoples who traditionally live on fish were able to catch thousands of salmon from areas only a few miles away from huge seal rookeries."[12] When only the native peoples, the seals, and other animals of the north were eating the fish, there was plenty for all. More than plenty—there was an abundance of fish. All this changed, however, with the development of a nonnative global fishing industry.

The modern fishing industry

Throughout history, coastal nations have fished, explored, and used the resources of their surrounding ocean waters: from people fishing from the beach and selling their catch at the local market, to groups of small boats fishing farther off the coast. But small, independent fishermen in poorly equipped boats are becoming a thing of the past. Nowadays, most fishing is done by large commercial fleets of modern, fully equipped ships. Often, the captain of a fishing vessel does not even own his boat. He and his crew are hired by large companies to work the boats.

The development of plastics has prompted giant technological advancements in the fishing industry. In recent years, giant plastic "drift nets" became a popular way for fleets to fish. They are also called "gill nets," because fish swim into them and entangle themselves by their gills. Drift nets are used mainly by Japan and Taiwan, although small fleets from other countries also use them.

Usually stretching more than 40 miles (64 km), the nearly invisible nets kill enormous amounts of sea life. Nicknamed "walls of death," drift nets don't just kill fish; they kill anything that comes in contact with them, including seals, sea turtles, dolphins, whales, seabirds, and immature tuna and salmon. Researchers from the University of Western Cape, South Africa, estimate that gill nets will kill at least eighty thousand seals every year.

Other technology has helped fishermen go farther and catch more fish. Most commercial fishing boats are equipped with radar and sonar. Sonar is particularly useful because it allows fishing boats to locate fish in the water. Radar enables boats to venture farther from shore while still staying in contact with coast guards and other rescue units, if

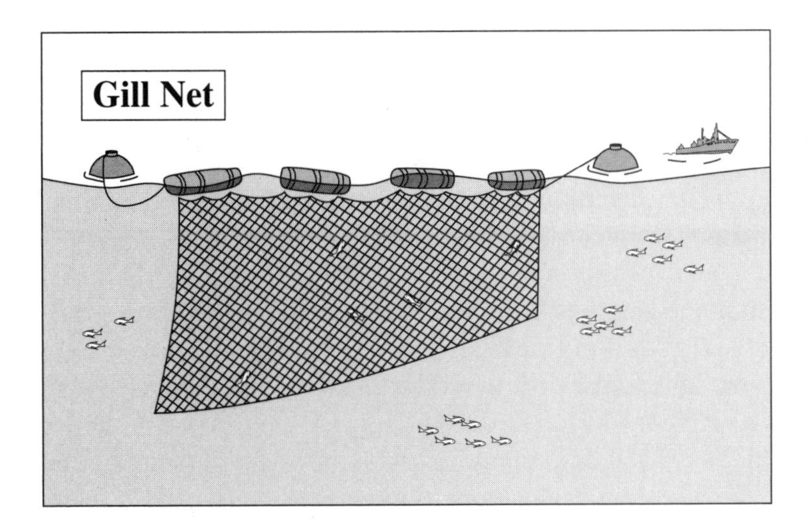

needed. Most fishing boats also come equipped with full refrigeration and processing facilities, allowing them to stay out for weeks at a time because any fish they catch stay "fresh."

Modern fishing and boating technology has made it possible for commercial fishermen to venture into areas they previously could only dream of going. No longer confined to local waters, modern fishing fleets can, and do, go anywhere on the globe. Norwegian fleets can catch cod in the waters off Canada, then ship it to Mexico or any other country. Through the development of modern techniques, huge numbers of fish can be caught, processed, and shipped to any part of the globe very rapidly.

Increased demand for fish

As the human population has increased around the world, so has the consumption of fish. The fact that there are more people on earth than ever before is not the sole reason for the increased consumption of fish. In the past few decades, more people have been exposed to fish as a food and have discovered they like it and want to purchase it. People who had never tasted ocean fish such as salmon and cod—for example, people living in landlocked areas like Oklahoma and Montana—are now able to eat ocean fish whenever they want. Fish used to be a rare treat for anyone not living by the ocean, but now it is almost always available anywhere in the world. If it's not available fresh, it can be found in the frozen-food section of a local grocery store.

Problems in the fishing industry

As the sealing industry declined, the fishing industry increased. In places such as Newfoundland and other parts of Canada, people had often both sealed and fished. In the summer they worked as fishers, and in the winter as sealers. By working at both jobs throughout the year, they were able to earn enough money to live on. When the sealing industry began collapsing, due to declining seal populations and public pressure, many northern peoples turned their attention exclusively to fishing.

Walls of Death

In the late 1980s, when driftnetting was in full force, more than 50,000 kilometers of drift nets were set *each night,* mostly by Japanese and other Asian fleets. Although there has been an international moratorium on driftnetting since 1992, there is strong evidence that drift nets are still being used in the South Pacific and Indian Oceans. As the conservation group Earthtrust reports in one of its 1998 newsletters, "DriftNetwork," the problem has by no means ended with the United Nations moratorium.

> Driftnetting is now widely considered to be *the most destructive fishing technology ever devised by humankind.* Combined mortalities to dolphins and other small cetaceans impacted by these nets were measured in the early 1990s to be in excess of several hundred thousand each year. In addition, millions of seabirds, tens of thousand of seals, thousands of sea turtles and great whales, and huge quantities of non-target fish species were killed in these nets each year. Pirate driftnetters—though less numerous than their formerly "legal" counterparts, continue these destructive practices.
>
> . . . Stopping pirate driftnetting—as commercial driftnetting has been stopped—would preserve marine resources and wildlife populations and offer much needed protection to the majority of fishermen who use viable economic and environmentally sustainable methods of fishing. It would also end the destruction caused by the loss of thousands of miles of nets each year. Lost nets, also called "ghost" nets, continue to "fish" as they float at sea until sinking under the weight of their victims or washing ashore where they entangle seals and seabirds.

Caught in a drift net noose, a Steller's sea lion struggles to free itself. Driftnetting puts many seals at risk.

Scientists agree that fishing by native and other northern peoples does not cause problems for the modern fishing industry. But overfishing by other groups has caused enormous problems.

Where have the fish gone?

For centuries, cod and capelin—a type of fish that cod eat—were plentiful throughout the North Atlantic. Newfoundland waters, for example, were home to huge amounts of capelin. According to an 1869 account by Captain R. B. McCrea, the local people ran into the water "up to their hips in fish and hauled them out in buckets."[13]

Capelin are near the bottom of the food chain. They are essential to the web of life in the entire North Atlantic Ocean. But in recent years, the capelin population has plummeted. Many reasons have been given, but the primary reason appears to be overfishing.

Overfishing has seriously upset the balance of the food chain and threatened other animal species that depend on fish for food.

Authors Fred Bruemmer and Brian Davies point out that

> Canada, in ignorance and folly, gave its capelin away to other nations, primarily to the Soviet Union, whose giant fleet scooped up the shoals of capelin and turned them into human food and into fish meal, protein-rich feed for pigs and chickens. The catch soared from 3,000 metric tons in 1970 to 370,000 metric tons in 1976. In a few years it was over. Capelin stocks crashed; seabirds perished; cod, deprived of their main prey, starved.[14]

With their main source of food gone, the cod population also plummeted. Cod all but disappeared from the waters of the North Atlantic.

Cod and capelin were not the only fish that suffered at the hands of gillnetters. Other North Atlantic fish populations also began showing drastic signs of decline. In a single night, each gillnetting boat could take in several tons of fish. Often the majority of the catch was tossed away—dead—if they were not the right kind of fish. Every year, hundreds of thousands of tons of fish were discarded in this way, simply because they weren't the type of fish the boat wanted, or because they wouldn't fetch a high market price. It became clear to many scientists that gillnetting was the most destructive and wasteful method of fishing ever invented.

In 1991, the United Nations declared an international ban on drift net fishing. Under its provisions, driftnetting was to be reduced to half by June 1992, and halted entirely by December 1992. The ban is still in effect. But scientists felt that it was already too late to save many fish populations.

In 1992, the cod population dropped dangerously low, and the Canadian government declared a two-year moratorium on all commercial cod fishing. Today, the cod population still shows little sign of recovery, and the ban has been extended indefinitely.

Many Canadian fishermen feel they have done all they can to help the cod and capelin recover. They are baffled as to why the fish are not rebounding and upset over losing their livelihood. Their problems are also compounded by "farmed fish" (fish grown in pools and pens) that are now

Fish farms like this trout farm have prevented the decimation of wild fish populations.

readily available to consumers. With farmed fish flooding the market, the price of fish has gone down. When "non-farming" fishermen are able to catch fish on the open seas, they often can't sell them for as much money as they used to. The Canadian fishermen are angry and frustrated. They want the problem fixed and have developed their own theories as to what is wrong.

Are seals to blame?

Many fishermen feel that cod populations are low because the seal population has become too large. The fishermen think the seals are eating all the fish.

Most scientists feel that the Canadian government, specifically the Department of Fisheries and Oceans, is to blame—not the seals. The scientists think the Canadian government ignored evidence that cod was being overfished, nearly to the point of extinction. They also think the government is now looking for a scapegoat—the seals—to cover up its own mistakes.

In 1992, the International Marine Mammal Association published the results of a forty-year study, which showed that only about 2 percent of the seal diet is composed of cod. The study concluded that "seals have played virtually no role in the depletion of northern cod and that culling seals would almost certainly not result in any particular benefit to the northern cod fishery."[15]

Scientists also point out that if seals were eating all the cod, then with their source of food vanishing, the seal population should be plummeting also—the way the cod population plummeted when the capelin disappeared. But seal populations in the North Atlantic, while not huge, are relatively stable.

Canadian government fishery scientists have conducted their own studies. "What happened to the fish stocks had nothing to do with the environment, nothing to do with seals. It (was) simply overfishing," says Ransom Myers, one of the Canadian scientists involved in the government study.[16]

Nevertheless, in the 1990s the fishing industry and the foundering sealing industry began seriously pressuring the Canadian government to resume commercial seal hunting and expand non-native quotas—the number of seals that commercial hunters can kill.

The "pest" of the seas?

Seals and the fishing industry have never gotten along very well. Although the general public thinks seals are cute and cuddly, fishermen think of them as destructive pests.

Fishermen claim that seals steal fish from nets and damage fishing gear in the process. Gray and harbor seals have also been known to bite fish out of nets. All of these actions cost the fishermen money.

Eat Fish? Not These Seals.

Not all seals make fish the primary staple of their diet. Some, like the crabeater seal in Antarctica, eat krill, tiny shrimp-like animals that are also eaten by baleen whales. Instead of the smooth teeth that other seals have—almost like a dog's—crabeater seals have serrated teeth like a saw. When they take in a mouthful of water full of krill, they clench their teeth and push their tongue against the inside of their mouth. The water escapes through the jagged edges of their teeth, but the krill stay behind, trapped in their mouth. Crabeater seals are the most populous seal species in the world today.

Although the leopard seals of Antarctica do eat fish, they are true predators and seem to prefer penguins, seal pups, and seabirds. Leopard seals are aggressive and can be quite vicious. They've been known to attack almost anything, including small boats carrying humans.

The most populous of the seal species, crabeater seals rely on krill instead of fish for food.

The New England Aquarium, a leader in researching declining fish populations, notes that in Maine,

> salmon growers report that seals kill or damage salmon in their pens, costing an estimated $1 million a year. (The total value of Maine-farmed salmon is about $40 million.) . . . Although salmon farmers employ deterrents such as double netting, acoustic seal scarers and life-size fiberglass models of

> killer whales (a natural predator), none are 100% effective. Studies have shown that regular net maintenance and other good farming practices do reduce predator loss.[17]

Many people say that seals are just a natural part of the business of fishing. They argue that just because seals eat fish is no reason to kill them. Fishermen argue that seals are overly destructive and make it very difficult for them to earn a living and support their families.

The hunt resumes

In 1995, the Canadian Fisheries minister, Brian Tobin, announced that commercial sealing would resume. He stated that there were 4.8 million seals in the North Atlantic, and that they were eating 142,000 tons of cod a year. The 1988 ban on commercial seal hunting had allowed an annual quota of one hundred thousand seals to be hunted and killed only by native and subsistence hunters. In 1996, the annual quota was nearly tripled, and allowed commercial non-native hunters. The seal hunt had resumed.

As a nation, Canada has always had the most seals. Consequently, Canada's harp seal hunt was always the largest, and certainly the most publicized and protested commercial seal hunt.

People opposed to resuming the hunt say that Canada's Department of Fisheries and Oceans failed to prove that the seal population actually increased as much as they said it did. They also point out that all scientific evidence indicates that seals are not responsible for the decline in cod populations.

The general public was not alone in raising an outcry. Ninety-seven biologists from fifteen countries angrily condemned Canada's move. They signed a petition stating:

> All scientific efforts to find an effect of seal predation on Canadian ground-fish have failed to show any impact. Overfishing remains the only scientifically demonstrated problem. If fishing closures continue, the evidence indicates that stocks will recover, and killing seals will not speed that process.[18]

To ignore public opposition and scientific evidence might seem foolhardy on the part of the Canadian government.

Hunters with clubs approach a group of northern fur seals. Seal hunts have resumed in areas where natural predators have not controlled seal populations.

But wildlife management is rarely easy for any government. Countries are composed of many different groups of people. In the case of Canada, commercial fishermen and sealers make up a significant portion of the population. The Canadian government is trying to keep them employed, and believes that resuming the seal hunt is the best way to accomplish that goal.

A new market demand for seals

Another reason for resuming the seal hunt is that a new market for seal parts has developed. Japan would like to buy 250,000 seals a year.

Japan and Asia have a booming aphrodisiac, or "sex potion," market. In the Orient, many people believe that consuming a seal's penis will enhance virility and sexual performance. Japan does not want the entire seal for its oil, meat, or fur pelt; Japan only wants the penises from male seals. In Chinese herbal-remedy shops, from Hong Kong to Vancouver and Calgary, seal penises (called *haiguo*) sell for $200 and up.

Critics of the hunt say that the Asian sex market is the real reason for resuming the hunt. They also point out that because the Asian sex market really only wants male genitals, nearly twice the reported numbers of seals are being killed. As Charles Enman, a journalist with the *Ottawa Citizen* reports,

> DFO [Canadian Department of Fisheries and Oceans] personnel found several sealing vessels carrying equal numbers of pelts and male seal genitals. Since male and female seals are impossible to distinguish until killed, this suggests that twice as many seals were harvested than reported, with the female animals simply being discarded.[19]

Scientists are also concerned that the lucrative Asian sex market is also fueling the killing of protected species. In a recent article in *Conservation Biology,* the authors report that "in 1994, fishers on the Galápagos Islands killed an undetermined number of Galápagos sea lions, a small population numbering 30–40,000, and sent a consignment of their penises to Japan."[20]

The general public, scientists, and environmental organizations have voiced anger over the actions of the Canadian government and Japan. The Canadian officials have

Sexual Benefits from Seals?

Scientists the world over have been concerned that the Asian sex market is encouraging the killing of protected seal species, particularly when a recently published molecular genetic study of 21 seal penises (all obtained from oriental shops in Asia and North America) revealed that only 11 of them came from harp seals.

But the authors of the study went on to reveal another curious fact: of the remaining 10 samples, 7 were not even from seals. Although they were being sold as "seal penis" the samples were from domestic cattle, African wild dog, or water buffalo.

Consequently, many people are questioning the Japanese—if the benefits don't come from seals, why are so many seals being killed?

denied that the Asian sex market is the reason for resuming the commercial seal hunt. They say that they are only trying to help the cod populations recover. But many people think the Canadian government is lying.

As David Lavigne, a marine biologist at the University of Guelph in Ontario, points out,

> One possibility is that a new company, North American Environmental Technologies Inc. (NAET) will be given the go-ahead to build a factory to process up to 250,000 seals for the "Asian Market." That NAET is promising to pay sealers twice as much for adult males than for females confirms the importance of seal penises for the aphrodisiac market in any attempt to revitalize Canada's seal hunt.[21]

Although seals are wild, free-ranging mammals, their fate in recent decades has been entirely in the hands of humans and governmental organizations. It remains to be seen how Canada and other nations will resolve these problems of wildlife management, fisheries management, public opinion, and unemployment.

4

Pollution and Habitat Destruction

AFTER SEAL POPULATIONS declined in the 1940s, seals somehow managed to come back from the brink of extinction once sealers left them alone. But they now face another, more dangerous threat at the hands of humans: pollution and habitat destruction.

Since 1987, there has been an unprecedented number of epidemics among seals. Seals are dying by the thousands. In only one year, more than eighteen thousand seals died in the Baltic Sea alone, all from a mysterious virus. The cause of the epidemics is unknown, but scientists have found high levels of pollutants known as PCBs in the tissues of the affected animals. They feel certain that pollution is the major cause of the viral epidemics that are killing seals and other marine creatures.

Other seals are nearly extinct because of habitat destruction. One example is the Mediterranean monk seal. Its habitat has been overrun with tourists and beachside resorts. There are no places left for it to breed, raise its young, or live.

Pollution and habitat destruction may doom seal populations much more effectively than hunting ever did.

Toxins on the planet

Human population is increasing all around the globe. Unfortunately, pollution has also increased along with the population. For centuries, humans gave little thought to disposal of their waste products. In the early twentieth century, when factories were being built, no one paid any attention to the sooty, choking smoke spewing from the smokestacks. And until recently, very few people paid attention to the ponds full of chemicals that surrounded some manufacturing factories, or to the toxins and polluted water that were being dumped into rivers, streams, and oceans, or just poured onto the ground.

In the past few decades, people have begun to realize just how dangerous pollution and chemicals can be. Most countries now have special departments in their government to deal with pollution and to enforce standards of water, air, and ground quality.

But pollution still remains an enormous global problem, and in some areas it is getting worse, not better. Disposing of toxic waste and polluted by-products can be very expensive. Many companies are more concerned about the cost than about the harmful effects that dumping has on the environment.

Sewage from a nearby factory flows from a drainage pipe onto a North Sea beach. It is often cheaper for companies to dump chemical waste than to treat it.

As Ginger Smith of the University of West Florida points out,

> Many companies dump wastes in the water to cut the cost of disposal in other manners. It is illegal to dump toxic wastes within United States waters but, as soon as you are out of them, anyone can dump anything. If you are caught illegally dumping toxic materials within U.S. waters you will be arrested and fined. For some of the companies it is cheaper to pay the fine and continue dumping toxic wastes close-by.[22]

In addition to toxic waste, oil is a major water pollutant. When people think of oil in the ocean, they usually think of giant oil spills—as when an oil tanker has an accident. But only about one-third of all ocean oil pollution comes from major oil spills or commercial transporting accidents. Almost half of the oil pollution in the ocean comes from polluted rivers flowing into the ocean. Agricultural runoff (containing fertilizers and pesticides) and sewage that has been discharged into a river are also major sources of chemical pollution in the oceans.

Because of the way water moves it its natural cycle, even pollutants on land find their way into the ocean. The oil dripping from a car parked outside a grocery store in Kansas will be washed into the water system by rain and eventually make its way to the ocean—just as surely as directly dumped chemicals.

Seals and the toxic food chain

Seals are particularly susceptible to toxic pollutants because they are near the top of the marine food chain.

When toxic waste is dumped in the ocean, it is immediately absorbed by plankton, zooplankton, and other tiny organisms—the foundation of the marine food chain. When an anchovy fish comes along and eats the plankton, it consumes a hefty dose of toxic waste. Then a larger capelin fish comes along and eats the anchovy. The capelin has just gotten a double dose of toxic waste—not only does the anchovy carry toxic chemicals in its body just from living in the water (like the plankton), but it has also just *eaten* something toxic, thereby putting even more toxic chemicals in its body. And the capelin has just eaten *it.*

The chain continues as a larger fish eats the capelin, and eventually a seal eats the larger fish. And all the time, the toxins are accumulating at a deadly rate. By the time the seal eats the fish, the toxic chemical levels are staggering.

Seals are doubly at risk because their blubber, besides nourishing them and keeping them warm, also stores toxins. With many animals, when they eat something bad, it passes through their digestive system in a matter of hours. But when seals consume toxins, the toxins do not pass out of their body through their digestive systems. Instead, the toxins enter their bloodstream and then remain in their body—held in fat storage by their blubber. With nursing cows, the effect becomes even more deadly. As they use up their blubber nursing their pups, the toxins are passed on to the seal pups through their mother's milk.

This toxic chain affects all animals near the top of the food chain: whales, dolphins, sharks, and humans. In this respect, humans and seals are alike. The same process occurs in us whenever *we* eat fish from polluted waters, or other foods contaminated with toxins.

According to the Marine Environmental Research Institute,

> Organochlorines (PCBs, DDT, dioxins, and chlorinated pesticides) are a special problem in the ocean environment because they bioaccumulate in marine mammals, the top predators along with humans, in the food chain. Seals, dolphins and whales have high levels of these chemicals in their blubber, and likewise, people who eat polluted seafood can also accumulate dangerous levels of PCBs.[23]

In addition to consuming food with high levels of toxicity, seals are also exposed to toxic chemicals every time they enter the water. Like plankton, they accumulate their own levels of toxicity without eating anything. In recent years, the effect of this deadly accumulation has become apparent.

Chemical deaths

Although seals constantly face the threat of renewed mass killings, their most serious threat, now and in the coming years, is still pollution.

An endangered Hawaiian monk seal nurses its newborn pup. Pollution poses a grave hazard to many seal populations.

The year 1986 marked the beginning of record-level die-offs of marine mammals and turtles. In every mass die-off, scientists consider toxic pollution to be a major contributing cause.

Marine mammals the world over are in trouble. The beluga whales of the St. Lawrence River have been among the hardest hit. They show much higher levels of lead, PCBs, mercury, and other deadly contaminants than the Arctic belugas do. The St. Lawrence belugas are suffering from bladder cancer, skin lesions, gastric ulcers, and genetic damage—making it highly unlikely that the population will even survive. From 1986 to 1996, so many belugas died off that less than four hundred remain.

Seals are not faring any better. Seal populations around the globe are showing the effects of pollution. Although the highest levels of contaminants in seal populations are showing up in Europe's North, Wadden, and Baltic Seas, species found in U.S. coastal waters are also in trouble. From 1992 to 1994, triple the usual number of seals were found dead or stranded on New York beaches. High levels of PCBs were found in all the seals tested.

A dead seal, a victim of oil pollution, is silent testimony to the effects of habitat destruction.

In California, the Marine Mammal Center has done postmortem studies on stranded California sea lions. Twenty percent of the animals tested had carcinomas, or cancerous growths. Carcinomas in laboratory animals, such as rats and fish, have been directly linked to exposure to PCBs and similar contaminants.[24]

How pollution kills

Scientists have noted that the biggest problem with exposure to toxic chemicals is the weakening effect that pollutants have on an animal's immune system—the body's system for fighting off disease and staying healthy. As toxins accumulate in a seal's body, it becomes more susceptible to disease. The result is that seals are now dying off in massive numbers from diseases that previously did not affect them. They're also dying off from mysterious viral infections and diseases that scientists are unfamiliar with.

The Marine Environmental Research Institute (MERI) points out that in 1987–88,

> More than 18,000 common (harbor) seals in the North and Baltic Seas died of a viral infection that resembles distemper. Scientists believe this epidemic, the largest die-off of seals in history, was fanned by industrial pollution in the North Sea. Common seals of the North Sea and the Wadden Sea are among the most PCB-contaminated marine mammals in the world.[25]

Recent scientific studies have confirmed these suspicions.

In 1994, Dr. Albert Osterhaus, a virologist at the University of Rotterdam, and a member of MERI's Advisory Board, provided the first evidence that exposure to PCBs and related organochlorine chemicals causes a severe immunodeficiency syndrome in captive harbor seals, leaving them vulnerable to disease. The seals in the study were fed PCB-contaminated fish from the Dutch Wadden Sea from a catch that was destined for human consumption.[26]

Double jeopardy for monk seals

The monk seal is already severely endangered. For years it has been ranked in the "Top Ten" list of the world's most endangered species, primarily due to habitat loss. Now pollution is adding to the Mediterranean monk seal's problem of survival.

There are very few monk seals left in the Mediterranean and adjoining Atlantic waters. The largest known population is in Mauritania, on the west coast of Africa. Early in the summer of 1997, the monk seals in the Mauritania colony started dying off dramatically. Researchers estimated that more than two-thirds of the known 310 seals died. They believe there are now only about 70 monk seals left in the Mauritania colony. Research indicates that the probable cause was a toxic algal bloom, also known as "red tide." Red tides can occur naturally and

The Mediterranean monk seal ranks among the world's ten most endangered species. Pollution has destroyed much of their habitat, leading to decreases in their population.

The Kardak Rocks: A "Country" for the Mediterranean Monk Seals?

For years, Turkey and Greece have been arguing over who owns certain uninhabited islands, or "rocks," in the Mediterranean and Aegean Seas. In recent years, both countries have claimed ownership and come perilously close to armed conflict. Now a third party, a group of Turkish ecologists, has entered the fray. Their aim is not to create another armed conflict, or even to claim the land for themselves. They want to make sure that the disputed rocks go to nobody but their true owners—the sea mammals threatened with extinction, the Mediterranean monk seals.

The ecologists have also presented the monk seals as a way to unify the people of Greece and Turkey, and they have already designed a flag for the new monk seal "country." The flag has no national colors on it, but rather, the likeness of a monk seal—illustrating the ecologists' viewpoint about who really owns the uninhabited rocks called "Kardak."

"Our aim was not to create another international crisis; we just wanted to pave the way to a peaceful approach to the dispute," Savas Emek, from the Izmir-based environmentalist group S.O.S. Akdeniz, said in a February 1996 article in the *Turkish Daily News.*

"There are hundreds of islets and rocks similar to Kardak in the Aegean Sea. As they are all uninhabited, they are natural wildlife reserves ideal for monk seals that chose the region for breeding. We want these places to remain as they are," said Emek.

Emek and other ecologists have stressed the urgent need for Greece and Turkey to resolve their differences. They state that the real losers in any military confrontation in the Mediterranean are the monk seals, whose survival depends on the existence of such uninhabited places.

"Greece and Turkey have to [work] together to provide Aegean wildlife with a secure and healthy environment," stated Emek.

make many marine mammals ill, but in this case scientists feel that the toxicity was worsened by pollution.

The best hope for survival of the Mediterranean monk seal lay in the health of the Mauritania colony, since it had the largest population. The die-off of the Mauritania colony has had a significant impact on the species' chances of survival.

Seals and oil

Pollution has a major effect on whales and other sea creatures. But seals have it even worse. They are creatures of both the sea *and* the land. In addition to pollution in the ocean, seals have to contend with land pollution every time they haul out of the water.

Oil spills are particularly devastating to seals. Not only is the oil in the water, but it also washes up on beaches. According to Peter Dyrynda and Rob Symberlist of the University of Wales,

"If the guns don't get you, the oil slicks will."

> Seals are very vulnerable with respect to oil pollution in that they have to spend much of their time at the surface of the water. They need to surface every few minutes to breath[e]. They regularly haul out onto beaches. During the course of an oil pollution incident they are at risk both when surfacing and when hauling out.[27]

When seals are exposed to oil, several things happen—none of them good. When their fur gets coated with oil, it no longer has the capacity to keep them insulated from the cold when they're in the water. They also can't dry off or get warm when they haul out of the water. A seal with oil in its fur is at enormous risk of getting chilled and dying of exposure.

Oil also gets into the seal's eyes, respiratory passages, and lungs, causing irritation and infections. If the infection is not treated, and many times even when it is treated, the seal will die.

Ghost nets and other deadly plastics

Pollution takes many forms, not just liquid chemicals or gooey oil. Seals and other marine mammals have to contend with many things in the ocean, or on the beaches, that do not belong there. A major pollutant that seals contend with is plastic.

The fishing industry dumps a lot of plastics into the ocean, often without intending to. Drift nets can break loose from the boat. Frequently, the broken drifting pieces are several miles long. Drift nets are made of thin monofilament nylon and are nearly invisible. Like deadly spider webs, these "ghost nets" drift for years, trapping and killing everything in their path. Scientists think ghost nets only stop killing when the weight of all the dead trapped animals causes the net to finally sink to the bottom.

Although drift nets were banned worldwide by the United Nations in 1992, there is overwhelming evidence that they are still being used. According to Earthtrust researchers,

> In 1993, driftnet vessels were found fishing in the North Pacific and there is ample indication that the Indian Ocean has become the new ocean of choice for large-scale driftnet fishing, mainly because enforcement in that body of water is minimal. In addi-

A sea lion struggles to free itself from a fish net. Seals and sea lions caught in nets face severe injury and death from drowning.

tion, the European Community permitted its member states to continue to fish in the North Atlantic, with nets over 2.5 kilometers in length, beyond the United Nations deadline.[28]

As long as drift nets (and their offspring, ghost nets) are in use, seals and other marine life will be in danger of entrapment and drowning. Before drift nets were officially banned, scientists determined that "more than 14,000 seals are drowned annually in the nets of the North Pacific drift net fishing vessels."[29]

Other plastics, such as six-pack holders, cups, bottles, fishing lines, and other nets, also float in the ocean and wash up on beaches. Cruise ships often dump their garbage overboard every night. All of this pollution poses health hazards for seals and other marine life. Seals usually die if they consume plastic. Others are found on beaches, tangled in plastic fishing lines and nets. If the plastic is not removed from its body, the seal will die.

No place to live

All seals face the problem of habitat destruction, as humans explore and exploit more of the earth. As Dr. Frances Gulland points out, "Loss of habitat can result directly in loss of species."[30]

Monk seals are more vulnerable to loss of habitat than almost any other species of seal because they are the only seals found in tropical seas. But warm turquoise waters and sandy beaches are the same places where humans like to live and vacation. Monk seals were once numerous in the Mediterranean and adjoining Atlantic, as well as the Caribbean and the Pacific near the Hawaiian Islands. But now the Caribbean monk seal is extinct, and the Mediterranean monk seal and Hawaiian monk seal are both endangered species.

Monk seals like to haul out on sandy beaches, the same sort of beaches that tourists love. They haul out to nap in the sun and relax. But like all seal species, monk seals also haul out to breed and raise their young. And this is where problems occur with the monk seal.

For reasons unknown to scientists, monk seals are unable to tolerate humans. They're completely rattled by most human activities—boating, jet skis, restaurants, and tourists. They don't want humans anywhere around them. Yet the very areas where they live and breed are populated and heavily visited by humans. California sea lions and a few other species that live in temperate waters face some of the same problems, but they're not bothered by human interference to the extent that monk seals are. California sea lions will share the beach with humans. Monk seals just leave, often abandoning their pups—*if* they've even been able to breed. If they don't haul out, they don't breed. And if humans are anywhere around a beach, they often won't haul out.

People used to think that if humans moved onto a beach, the monk seals would just find some other beach. But it has become clear in the last few decades that they don't do this. So many beaches have been developed that not many secluded beaches are left, and monk seals like their own beaches. Although they do sometimes relocate themselves, they don't seem to transplant very well.

The Caribbean monk seal is already extinct, but in the Hawaiian Islands, reserves have been set aside for the monk seals. Although the Hawaiian monk seals are not doing well, their numbers are not declining drastically. Scientists estimate that about twelve hundred Hawaiian monk seals remain.

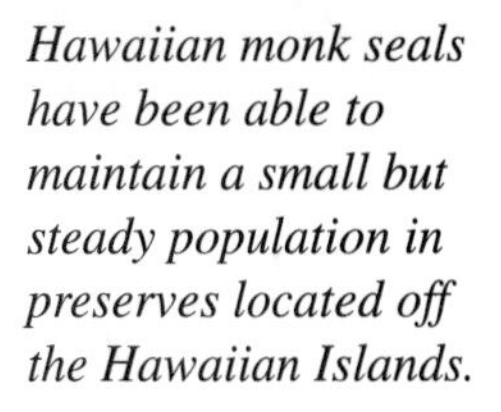

Hawaiian monk seals have been able to maintain a small but steady population in preserves located off the Hawaiian Islands.

The Mediterranean monk seals face a tougher battle. Many countries border the Mediterranean, and few of them are able to agree on how to best protect the monk seal, if at all. Fishermen view the seal as a competitor for the fish supply and don't want to see it protected. Scientists think there are now only about two hundred Mediterranean monk seals remaining in the world. Some of these remaining monk seals have relocated themselves from warm sandy beaches into rocky, partially submerged caves. Although the caves afford them some much needed seclusion, their pups aren't doing as well. Scientists speculate that cave living and lack of sunlight is to blame.

Monk seals living in tropical paradises are not the only ones facing the loss of their habitats. Seals in the polar regions are also at risk for habitat destruction. Although relatively few people live in the polar regions, many corporations have oil, gas, and mineral drilling operations there. All polar animals risk destruction of their habitat due to drilling operations. Oil spills pose the greatest danger to seals in the polar regions. The garbage that any human settlement creates, much of it plastics, and the disruption that human activities bring also pose problems for seals. The drilling companies say they will be careful of environmental damage, but many people would like to see all polar drilling and mining operations shut down. They feel that the polar environment is too fragile, and that, once damaged, it will never recover.

"Natural" habitat destruction

Seals also face the same naturally occurring habitat destruction that all other animals on the planet face, including humans. Storms, high tides, and other weather conditions can have devastating effects on seal populations. Every few years, the Pacific Ocean creates a huge current of warm water that wells off the west coast of South America. As this warm current, called "El Niño," swells through the Pacific, it disrupts weather patterns and creates rougher seas. El Niño seasons are particularly hard on seals.

El Niño greatly affected the sea lion population in places such as San Miguel Island off the California coast. About six thousand sea lion pups died on this island in the first few months of the 1997–98 El Niño.

Pups and young seals are hardest hit during an El Niño year. Under the best of conditions, pups are left on their own while their mothers forage in the sea for food. Usually, the mother is gone for about a week, then returns to nurse her pup before heading out to forage again.

El Niño: Should Humans Help?

Seals don't always find trouble at the hands of humans. Sometimes they run into trouble all on their own, and people actually try to help them out.

During an El Niño year, like 1997–98, a huge body of warm water swells through the Pacific, altering weather conditions around the globe, creating giant storms with larger waves and stiffer winds, and wreaking havoc on marine life.

Young California sea lions are particularly hard hit during El Niño years. In 1998, they washed up on California beaches by the hundreds. And when a seal or sea lion washes up on a beach, SeaWorld and other marine mammal rescue centers spring into action. At least 160 animals were rescued by SeaWorld in just January and February alone.

But federal wildlife officials have suggested that saving individual sea lions is not in the best interest of nature, or even the species as a whole. They feel that these beached animals aren't necessarily born to survive. The population of California sea lions is growing phenomenally—by about 10 percent yearly—and now stands at 180,000. The officials claim that the die-off due to El Niño is part of a natural cycle that keeps the seal and sea lion populations in check. The government estimates that 100 percent of the northern fur seal pups and 80 percent of the sea lion pups will die in 1998, all because of El Niño. Large die-offs are also expected for year-old harbor and elephant seals.

Even the rescuers admit that their efforts are driven as much by public pressure as by concern for the animals' welfare. In the February 25, 1998, *San Diego Union-Tribune,* Jim Antrim, SeaWorld's curator, said, "We do it as a humanitarian gesture, but there are some issues that arise that can be bothersome." He notes that people have pushed seals and sea lions out of their natural habitats and polluted their waters—the southern California coastline is the most densely populated coastline in the United States. "Maybe we feel a little collective guilt and owe them a rescue mission every once in a while."

During El Niño conditions, the water warms, often by as much as five degrees. Most species of fish, particularly the ones that seals prey upon, like colder water. As the water warms, the fish venture farther and deeper, seeking colder water. When seal mothers leave the rookery to forage for both themselves and their pups, the fish are no longer relatively close to shore. The seals have to swim much farther and dive much deeper than they would in a non–El Niño year. Consequently, the nursing cows are gone from the rookery longer than usual, and even then they often catch fewer fish. The pups are left alone for longer periods of time, without food. When the mothers do return, they have expended more energy, yet not really increased their milk supply. So after being left alone without food for longer periods of time, the pups still don't receive the extra nourishment they need. During the 1982–83 El Niño season, nearly 60 percent of the northern fur seal pups on the Channel Islands off the coast of California did not survive.

Pups and young seals are also affected by storms. High waves can wash pups right out of a rookery. Young seals find it hard to survive storm conditions because they lack the body size and strength to battle waves and find food.

Environmental sentinels

As top predators in the marine ecosystem, seals are ideal sentinels for the health of the entire ecosystem. If seals have high levels of PCBs in their bodies, poor reproduction rates, and poorly functioning immune systems, then all other marine species will soon exhibit the same symptoms. It is only a matter of time. And as top predators in the terrestrial *and* marine ecosystems, humans will also soon show the same symptoms.

How people and governments around the globe solve the problems of pollution is of vital interest to every living thing on the planet in the years to come.

5

The Future

IN THE PAST few decades it has become apparent that mass killings at the hands of sealers, and stresses from the effects of pollution, have proved too much for several seal species. Some species have rebounded and held steady, but for others the future is far from certain.

Legislation to protect seals

In an effort to remedy the situation and help depleted species, nations began enacting legislation in the 1970s to make it illegal for people to harm, harass, or kill any species that were considered depleted or in danger of extinction. In the United States, the Marine Mammal Protection Act of 1972 is one such law currently being used to protect seal populations. It mandates that all marine mammals, including seals, be left alone. It is illegal to harass or hurt any marine mammal. The Marine Mammal Protection Act also controls seals that are in zoos or amusement parks and limits how many animals may be taken from the wild for such purposes.

The Endangered Species Act also offers protection to seals, although a population or species is usually severely depleted before it gets the additional protection of this law. Other nations have enacted similar legislation that offers protection to animals within their borders.

Nations around the globe also realized that they needed to do more than just protect animals within their own borders. On July 1, 1975, the Convention on the International Trade in Endangered Species (CITES) was held. The result was a global treaty that governs all animal trade. More than 135 countries currently participate in the CITES, and membership is expanding. The CITES recognizes that international trade often influences the hunting of a species. For example, elephants in Africa are killed because people in Asia want their ivory, and seals in Canada are killed because people in Japan want body parts. The CITES tries to control this type of trade so that a species will not be wiped out because of international market forces.

Every international treaty and protection act helps seals and other species. But legislation is no guarantee of a species' survival. Typically, in the United States, a species must be severely depleted before it receives the benefit of the Endangered Species Act. By the time a seal species makes it onto an "endangered" list, it has often suffered a series of mishaps. One more mishap—like an oil spill offshore of its rookery, or a pollution-caused infection—will push it right into extinction.

Private groups like Greenpeace, the World Wildlife Fund, and the International Fund for Animal Welfare have helped to raise public awareness of the plight of seals. They hope that by increasing public concern, seal species won't need to be on an "endangered" list before they receive protection. Few of these groups challenge the right of Inuit, Eskimo, and other native peoples to hunt seals for

Extinction Is Forever

For the Caribbean monk seal, there is no future. Although the U.S. Fish and Wildlife Service retains the Caribbean monk seal on its official list of endangered species, no recovery efforts are being made. The last recorded Caribbean monk seal was killed off the coast of Key West, Florida, in 1922. The last reliable report of a sighting occurred in 1952, when a pair of seals were spotted. Organized searches have failed to find any trace of living Caribbean monk seals, and scientists believe that the species has been extinct since around 1960.

their own use; rather, it is the commercial killing of millions of seals by organized outfitters that wildlife organizations oppose.

Vanishing legislation

Many people assume that because legislation is in place, a particular animal species is safe and they can turn their attention to other things. Unfortunately, this is rarely the case. Even with legislation, a species has no guarantee of protection. Laws work only if nations choose to retain and enforce them. As governments change, animal protection treaties change also.

The economic marketplace also influences a nation's choice of whether or not to enforce legislation. For example, Canadian harp seals appear to be protected from mass commercial killings only if there is no market demand for seal products. But even if one market disappears, such as the market for sealskin coats, a new one may spring up. The Canadian government has also fought very hard to keep harp seals from being a CITES-regulated species. Many member nations of the CITES would like to control the hunting of harp seals and deplore Canada's actions.

Harp seals protected by legislation?

By 1987, Canada's commercial harp seal hunt had been going on for centuries. Yet on December 30 of that year, Canada's then minister of fisheries and oceans, Tom Siddon, announced a ban on the hunting of baby harp seals. Environmental and scientific groups had submitted countless briefs dealing with the science, ethics, and economics of sealing. But ultimately, it was public sentiment that decided the issue. The Royal Commission recommended that the ban be put in place because "the commercial hunting of the pups of the harp seal (whitecoats) and hooded seals (bluebacks) is widely unacceptable to the general public and should not be permitted."[31]

Environmental groups and most of the general public were pleased. As Brian Davies, founder of the International Fund for Animal Welfare (IFAW), recounts, "When I

A 1978 photo shows Greenpeace members protesting the slaughter of seals. Public outcry led to a commercial hunting ban in Canada in 1988.

opened my newspaper on January 1, 1988, and read the headline, 'Canada Bans Baby Seal Hunt,' it was a dream come true."[32]

Less than ten years later, a new government and a new minister of fisheries and oceans were in place. Brian Davies continues, "But in the spring of 1996 the dream was shattered. A combination of new, politically motivated government subsidies and favorable ice conditions left the ice floes off the east coast of Canada red with the blood of more than a quarter of a million brutally slaughtered seals."[33]

Accelerating extinction

Extinction has always been a natural feature of life on this planet. However, with the unprecedented expansion of the human race, more and more species are declining because of loss of habitat, killing, and pollution. Humans are no longer innocent bystanders witnessing natural extinction; they are actively driving the extinction bulldozer. For most species, including seals, extinction rarely results from one large catastrophic event; it usually happens after a series of events, nearly all of which could have been prevented, because most are caused by humans.

Pribilof Islands fur seals

The northern fur seals of Alaska's Pribilof Islands are a good example of a species suffering one mishap on top of another—until extinction looms.

From 1908 to 1910, more than 4 million fur seals were killed on the Pribilof Islands. Very few species can withstand the loss of 4 million individuals in three years, in addition to millions more in previous years. The Pribilof fur seals were nearly wiped out. People finally recognized just how endangered the fur seals were. As a result, the Hay-Elliott Fur Seal Treaty was ratified in 1911 by Japan, China, Russia, and the United States, giving the seals a chance to recover.

Images of wide-eyed baby harp seals prompted the public to protest commercial hunting of seal pups.

At the signing of the Hay-Elliott treaty, there were about two hundred thousand fur seals left on the Pribilof Islands, which represented nearly all the northern fur seals in the world. The seals started to rebound a bit, but not as much as scientists hoped. In 1957, the treaty was revised, making the Pribilof Islands a special government reservation.

But high levels of toxins started showing up in the Pribilof Islands fur seals. The effects of the contaminants not only weakened their immune systems, making them more susceptible to disease, but also affected their reproductive capabilities.

In 1988, the Pribilof Islands' stock of northern fur seals was declared "depleted" but not officially "endangered." Being designated as "depleted" means that the population has fallen below its optimum level. Since then, conservation efforts have been in place to help the stock recover.

Northern fur seals gather in a rookery at St. Paul Island in the Pribilof Islands. The depletion of the northern fur seal resulted in efforts to increase their numbers.

Conservation efforts on the Pribilof Islands

Northern fur seals are found throughout the north Pacific. They range from Alaska to Baja California. Mostly they're found in Alaskan waters, but in the winter they migrate south toward Baja. More than two-thirds of all northern fur seals live and breed on the Pribilof Islands—which is what makes the Pribilof Islands fur seals so important. This one group represents the majority of the species. If something happens to the Pribilof Islands fur seals, the whole species of northern fur seals is in trouble.

To date, the government conservation plan for the Pribilof Islands fur seals has relied heavily on watching, researching, and reporting what is happening. The plan lists two objectives. One is to "expand research or management programs to meet population trends and detect natural or human-related causes of changes in the Pribilof Islands northern fur seal population and habits essential to its survival and recovery." The other objective is to "assess and avoid or mitigate possible adverse effects of human-related activities on or near the Pribilof Islands and other habitat essential to northern fur seals throughout their range."[34]

Toxic contamination still remains a problem. Although conservation measures and protection are in place, the fur seals of the Pribilof Islands still show very high levels of toxins in their bodies. They are not reproducing normally. Many of the females don't get pregnant at all, and those that do have pups that are sick and don't survive.

Scientists at the National Marine Fisheries Service think that much of the toxic pollution is picked up when the seals migrate southward, along the California coast. In a bulletin dealing with the conservation plan for the Pribilof fur seals, the service states that

> since northern fur seals migrate down the coast of California to San Miguel Island and forage along the way, there is significant potential for the contaminants to impact northern fur seals. Illegal discharge of petroleum products from the increasing vessel traffic is also a matter of concern.[35]

Although the seals' breeding place and rookeries may be protected, there's not much that researchers in Alaska can do when the seals migrate and are exposed to oil and toxins off the coast of California.

Endangered Seals in U.S. Waters

The U.S. Fish and Wildlife Service, the government organization in charge of marine mammals and endangered species, lists several species of seals found in U.S. waters that are considered endangered.

Guadalupe fur seals

Commercial sealing in the late eighteenth and early nineteenth centuries left the Guadalupe fur seal population at an endangered level. By 1825, the seal had completely vanished from the waters of southern California. Commercial hunting still continued in the waters off Mexico until 1895. But where other populations managed to rebound once they were protected or left alone, the Guadalupe fur seal population has not. After more than 100 years to "come back," the Guadalupe fur seal is still an endangered species.

Hawaiian monk seals

The Hawaiian monk seal has been officially listed as endangered since 1976. Most of its habitat range has been lost to human expansion. Although the species has been protected for several decades, it still is not recovering. For reasons not entirely known to scientists, the Hawaiian monk seal population is declining.

Steller's sea lions

In 1990, Steller's, or northern, sea lions were listed as threatened throughout their range, which is primarily throughout the Gulf of Alaska and the Aleutian Islands, although they also range as far as eastern Russia. There are still several thousand animals in the population, but their number is declining rapidly and dramatically. In the late 1970s, the population was about 248,000. In 1989, it was about 116,000. And in 1994, only about 67,100 were counted in the U.S. population. Toxin levels were found to be high in the sea lions' blubber.

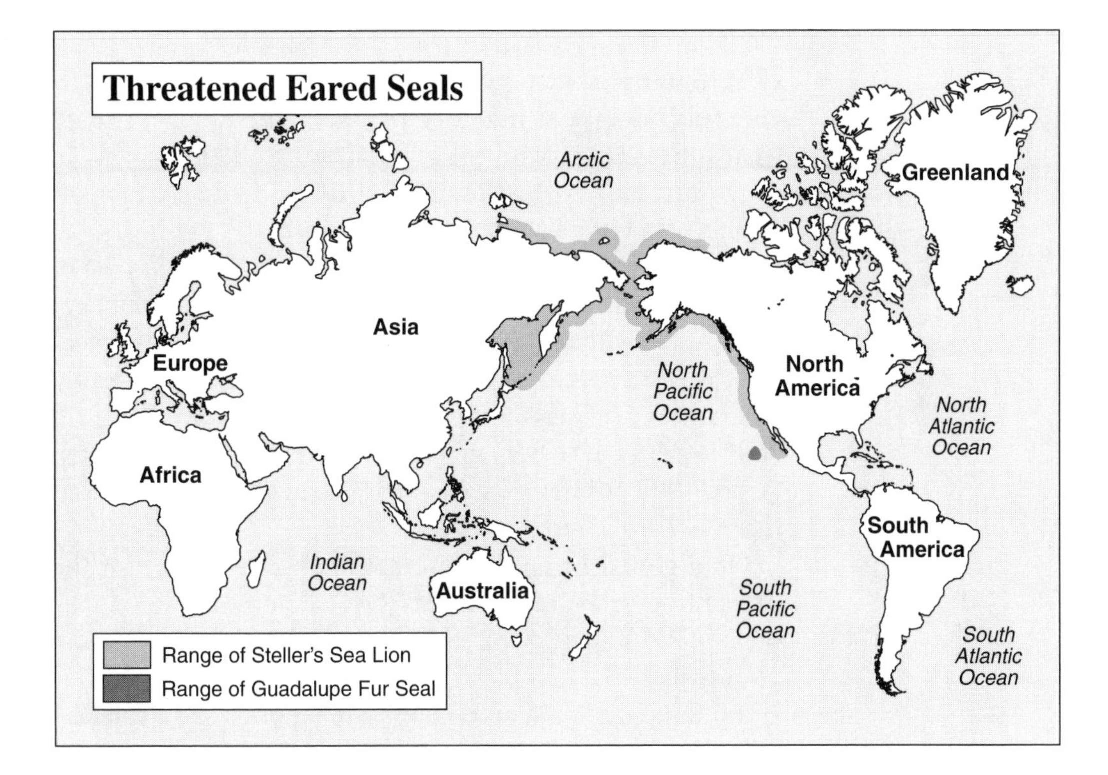

Controlling global pollution?

With resources disappearing, fish populations dying off, and marine mammals stranding on beaches, nations are taking a closer look at how they treat the ocean. In an effort to focus attention on the ocean's resources and problems, the United Nations declared 1998 "The Year of the Ocean."

In the past decades, most nations have developed their own plans for dealing with marine pollution and the accompanying threats to wildlife. And most nations are already actively trying to implement antipollution measures. "The Year of the Ocean" gives nations a way to pool their knowledge and formulate global plans. In 1998, more than three hundred international conferences were held around the globe, all of them under the auspices of "The Year of the Ocean," and all of them designed to promote understanding of the marine environment.

In the 1970s, the United States began enacting legislation designed to curb pollution. The Federal Water Pollution

Control Act, which later became the Clean Water Act (CWA), aims to restore and maintain the chemical, physical, and biological integrity of the waters in the United States. Besides providing for monitoring and management programs, the CWA also makes it illegal to discharge pollutants into U.S. waters without a permit.

In addition to the CWA, the United States has many other pollution-control laws in place: the Coastal Zone Management Act; the National Estuary Program; the Marine Protection, Research, and Sanctuaries Act; and the Oil Pollution Act, which was passed as a result of the *Exxon Valdez* oil spill in Alaskan waters in 1989. The Ocean Dumping Ban Act of 1998 prohibits the dumping of sewage sludge and industrial wastes into the ocean.

On a global level, the International Convention for the Prevention of Pollution from Ships (commonly known as the MARPOL Treaty) attempts to control marine pollution worldwide.

Although national and international pollution legislation will benefit seals, the effects of decades' worth of dumping in the oceans will be felt for quite some time. But throughout the world, the realization is dawning that the oceans are not a dumping ground. Scientists hope the realization is not coming too late.

The future for Hawaiian monk seals

For years, scientists have been baffled by the failure of the Hawaiian monk seals to thrive. Habitat loss and PCB contamination certainly contribute to the problem, but overall, Hawaiian monk seals don't have it very bad when it comes to habitat and toxins. For decades, they've had protected reserves, and the waters surrounding the Hawaiian Islands are some of the cleanest in the world.

Recently, scientists have discovered that poor mating practices may be the major contributing factor in the decline of the species. Male Hawaiian monk seals will often mob a female, severely injuring her when they attempt to mate. The injuries often kill the female—if not directly on the spot, then later. With severe injuries, the female is not able to forage and feed. And with bleeding wounds, she is also more susceptible to attack by tiger sharks. If she does manage to survive the wounds and actually give birth, she is usually too weak to take care of her pup, and they both end up perishing.

Scientists are baffled by this mobbing behavior on the part of the Hawaiian monk seals. They speculate that with so few animals remaining, the males have developed more aggressive behavior so they can obtain a female for mating. But the males' aggressive fighting also mortally injures the remaining females. As the number of female Hawaiian monk seals drops even lower, the behavior of the male seals becomes even more aggressive. In a natural attempt to reproduce their own species, the Hawaiian monk seals are killing themselves off.

To try and prevent the male Hawaiian monk seals from killing their remaining females, the Monk Seal Project has come up with an unusual conservation plan. They are attempting to chemically lower the testosterone level of the

The mating habits of the Hawaiian monk seal have undermined efforts to increase their population.

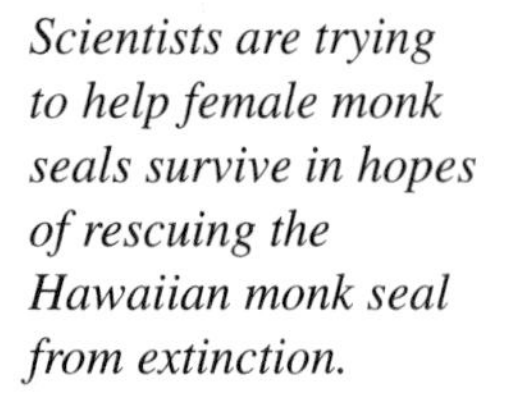

Scientists are trying to help female monk seals survive in hopes of rescuing the Hawaiian monk seal from extinction.

most violent males, in order to calm them down so that normal mating can occur. If the plan is successful, more females will give birth—and produce more female pups. Scientists believe that with more female monk seals available for mating, the males' mobbing behavior will diminish.

So far, initial tests done at the Sea Life Park in Honolulu have worked, and scientists are hopeful the experiment will be successful in the wild.

Alternatives to sealing

Many conservation groups realize the importance of seal hunting to Arctic native peoples, not only as a way of life, but also as a way of earning critically needed cash. If seal hunting is entirely banned, how will these native peoples, who depend on it for their living, survive?

To help solve this dilemma, the Sea Shepherd Conservation Society has proposed an alternative to sealing: brushing out the molted hairs from live seal pups, and using them to make sweaters, sleeping bags, and other cold-weather gear.

A Sea Shepherd press release of 1993 reported that workers were able to brush large quantities of seal hair from living seals. "The seals actually seemed to enjoy the brushing, which probably relieved the itching of the molting stage."[36]

Since 1994, the Sea Shepherd Conservation Society has made seal brushing an annual research project. They are hoping to set up manufacturing facilities and provide seal hunters with an alternative to killing the seals, as well as a much needed source of income.

A last hope for endangered species?

In the last decade, many humans have used sophisticated reproduction technology as a way of starting a family. Now these same techniques are being used to help save endangered species. Reproductive techniques—such as artificial insemination, in-vitro (test-tube) fertilization, surrogate parents, and frozen storage of embryos—just may offer endangered species a second chance. For some species, the new procedures may offer their last hope for survival.

Artificial reproduction can dramatically increase the population of an endangered species. Sperm can be removed from a fit male and be preserved and shipped around the world to impregnate many females within the species. It is also easier to ship an animal's cells than the entire animal.

The new procedure can also help physically or behaviorally handicapped animals to reproduce. Although scientists are not currently using this method with Hawaiian monk seals, artificial insemination is something they may consider if lowering the testosterone levels doesn't work.

Biomedical reproductive techniques are very time-consuming and difficult. Scientists must first know the complete reproductive cycle of the animal involved. With endangered species, this can be a difficult process. Dr. David Wildt, of the Smithsonian National Zoological Park in Washington, D.C., and his colleagues have worked out some of the problems by studying the domestic cat. As Dr. Wildt explains,

> In-vitro fertilization requires an amazing amount of time in the laboratory and a lot of expensive and specialized equipment. Working together, our graduate students at the National

Zoo were able to solve most of the problems for the domestic cat effectively. Still the work required two years of research, which is a long time when trying to produce a technique applicable to endangered species.[37]

The work with in-vitro fertilization holds other possibilities. For example, embryos from an endangered species might be implanted in a female of a related species who would then give birth. This "surrogate parenting" would be valuable when the females of an endangered species are somehow unfit for giving birth to healthy young, but are nevertheless able to produce viable ova for an embryo.

Continued research in zoos and in the wild may allow scientists to find ways to keep endangered seals and sea lions alive.

Zoos might also freeze embryos of the captive animals whose species is threatened in the wild. Although saving

the natural habitat of endangered species is the first priority of wildlife researchers, such reproductive techniques might provide another safeguard against extinction.

Seals and humans forever?

Throughout the centuries, seals and humans have inhabited the globe together. Humans are more than just top predators, and seals are more than just animals. Both are linked together in the complex ecosystem called "earth." The fate of the seal rises and falls in the hands of humans, just as humans hold the key to their own future.

In 1928, author Henry Beston offered a suggestion for coexisting in a complex ecosystem:

> We need another and a wiser and perhaps a more mystical concept of animals. . . . We patronize them for their incompleteness, for their tragic fate of having taken form so far below ourselves. And therein we err, and greatly err. For the animal shall not be measured by man. In a world older and more complete than ours they move finished and complete, gifted with extensions of the senses we have lost or never attained, living by voices we shall never hear. They are not brethren, they are not underlings; they are other nations, caught with ourselves in the net of life and time, fellow prisoners of the splendour and travail of the earth.[38]

Notes

Chapter 1: The Basics About Seals

1. Dorothy Hinshaw Patent, *Seals, Sea Lions, and Walruses.* New York: Holiday House, 1990, p. 9.

2. Jacques-Yves Cousteau and Philippe Diole, *Diving Companions: Sea Lion–Elephant Seal–Walrus.* Garden City, NY: Doubleday, 1974, p. 38.

3. Cousteau and Diole, *Diving Companions,* p. 39.

4. John Bonnett Wexo, *Seals, Sea Lions, and Walruses.* Mankato, MN: Creative Education, 1987, p. 17.

5. Cousteau and Diole, *Diving Companions,* p. 33.

Chapter 2: Hunting Seals

6. Cousteau and Diole, *Diving Companions,* p. 202.

7. Randall R. Reeves, Brent S. Stewart, and Stephen Leatherwood, *The Sierra Club Handbook of Seals and Sirenians.* San Francisco: Sierra Club, 1992, p. 32.

8. "History," Canadian Sealers Association, www.sealers.nf.ca/history.htm.

9. Vassili Papastavrou, *Wildlife at Risk: Seals and Sea Lions.* New York: Bookwright Press, 1992, p. 19.

10. Quoted in Janet Herrlinger and Peter Erdman, "The Baby Seal Trade," gurukul.ucc.american.edu/ted/BABYSEAL.htm.

11. Herrlinger and Erdman, "The Baby Seal Trade."

Chapter 3: Fighting for Fish

12. Eric S. Grace, *Sierra Club Wildlife Library: Seals.* San Francisco: Sierra Club, 1991, p. 61.

13. Quoted in Fred Bruemmer and Brian Davies, *Seasons of the Seal.* Buffalo, NY: Firefly Books, 1997, p. 91.

14. Bruemmer and Davies, *Seasons of the Seal,* p. 91.

15. Quoted in Andrew Christie, "The Tragic Return to Commercial Sealing," Sea Shepherd Conservation Society, www.seashepherd.org/se/setback.html.

16. Quoted in David Lavigne, "The Sudden Ecologists," *BBC Wildlife,* vol. 14, no. 1, January 1996, p. 57, www.imma.org/sudden.html.

17. "The Growing Seal Population in the Gulf of Maine," Fact Sheet 3, New England Aquarium, whale.wheelock.edu/whalenet-stuff/seal_factsheet3.html.

18. Quoted in Lynda Hurst, "Experts Question Slaughter of Seals," *Vancouver Sun,* February 2, 1996, envirolink.org/arrs/news/experts_oppose.html.

19. Quoted in "Canadian 1997 Seal Hunt Kill Totals In," Sea Shepherd Conservation Society, www.seashepherd.org/se/seca97.html.

20. "Market for Seal Penises Prompting Unregulated Hunting of Protected Species," SeaWeb Ocean Update, April 1998, from S. Malik et al., "Pinniped Penises in Trade: A Molecular-Genetic Investigation," *Conservation Biology,* vol. 11, no. 6, pp. 1365–1374, www.seaweb.org/16update/seal.html.

21. Lavigne, "The Sudden Ecologists," p. 57.

Chapter 4: Pollution and Habitat Destruction

22. Ginger Smith, "Water Pollution," University of West Florida, December 8, 1995, science.cc.uwf.edu/sh/curr/waterpollution/water.htm.

23. "Research: Marine Environmental Research Institute Chronology of Marine Mammal Die-offs with Selected References," Marine Environmental Research Institute, downeast.net/nonprof/meri/res.html.

24. Dr. Frances Gulland, "Environmental Sentinels: The

Canary in the Coal Mine," from an address to the American Veterinary Medical Association, www.tmmc.org/canaries.htm.

25. "Research: Marine Environmental Research Institute Chronology of Marine Mammal Die-offs with Selected References."

26. "Research: Marine Environmental Research Institute Chronology of Marine Mammal Die-offs with Selected References."

27. Peter Dyrynda and Rob Symberlist, "Sea Empress Oil Spill: Marine Mammals," University of Wales Swansea School of Biological Sciences, www.swan.ac.uk/\biosci/empress/mammals/mammals.htm.

28. "Earthtrust's 'DriftNetwork' Program," Earthtrust, www.earthtrust.org/dnw.html.

29. "Gill Nets," *UWC Enviro Facts,* University of Western Cape, South Africa, www.botany.uwc.ac.za/EnvFacts/gill/index.htm.

30. Gulland, "Environmental Sentinels: The Canary in the Coal Mine."

Chapter 5: The Future

31. Quoted in Bruemmer and Davies, *Seasons of the Seal,* p. 10.

32. Bruemmer and Davies, *Seasons of the Seal,* p. 10.

33. Bruemmer and Davies, *Seasons of the Seal,* p. 10.

34. "North Pacific Fur Seal Conservation Efforts," Marine Mammal Protection Act Home Page, www.nmfs.gov/tmcintyr/depleted/frsealre.html.

35. "Final Conservation Plan for the Pribilof Islands Northern Fur Seal," *North Pacific Fur Seal,* National Marine Fisheries Service, 1993, www.nmfs.gov/tmcintyr/depleted/furseal. html.

36. "Sea Shepherd Seal Campaigns," Sea Shepherd Conservation Society, www.seashepherd.org/actions/acseal.html.

37. Quoted in Marc Bretzfelder, "Artificial Reproduction: A Last Hope for Some Endangered Species," Smithsonian News Service, February 1989, www.si.edu/natzoo/zooview/newsserv/artrepro.htm.

38. Henry Beston, *The Outermost House.* New York: Penguin, 1928, p. 25.

Glossary

blubber: A thick layer of fat just under the skin of seals and other sea mammals.

bulls: Male seals.

carnivore: An animal that eats meat.

cows: Female seals.

die-off: A sudden sharp population decline that is not caused by direct human activity such as hunting.

DNA: Short for deoxyribonucleic acid, DNA is the "chemical blueprint for life" found in the chromosomes of every living creature's body cells.

drift net: A fishing net made of nearly invisible monofilament nylon, usually many miles long. Sometimes called "gill nets," they entangle and kill anything in their path, including seals, turtles, whales, dolphins, and seabirds.

eared seals: Pinnipeds in the scientific order Otariidae (fur seals and sea lions), which have small, visible, external ears.

endangered: Likely to become extinct if actions are not taken to help the species.

extinct: No longer in existence.

flippers: The wide, flat appendages on animals that are used for swimming. Somewhat like human arms and legs, seals have four flippers.

floe: A large sheet, or piece, of ice that floats on the surface of the water.

ghost net: A drift net that has broken away from a fishing boat and floats in the ocean on its own, trapping and killing sea life.

guard hairs: The long, coarse hairs on a seal's pelt that support and cover the finer, softer underfur.

haul out: To leave the ocean and return to the land to rest, breed, or raise their young.

hemoglobin: Special protein cells that store oxygen in the blood.

krill: Tiny shrimp-like animals eaten by many marine mammals.

mammals: Animals that are warm-blooded, nurse their young, and whose skin is usually covered with fur or hair.

mate: To engage in breeding to produce offspring.

myoglobin: Special protein cells that store oxygen in the muscles.

PCBs: Short for "polychlorinated biphenyls." Poisonous chemicals used in industry and manufacturing, PCBs are toxic to all living things.

pinnipeds: A group of marine mammals that belong to the scientific order Pinnipedia. Seals, fur seals and sea lions, and walruses make up the order Pinnipedia.

predator: An animal that hunts other animals for its food.

prey: An animal that is hunted and caught for food.

pups: Baby seals.

rebound: To increase in numbers after a population decrease.

rookery: A place where large numbers of animals gather to mate and raise their young.

sealer: A person who engages in sealing, the hunting and killing of seals.

subsistence: Taking only the amount that is necessary for survival.

true seals: Pinnipeds in the scientific order Phocidae, which have no visible external ear.

virus: A submicroscopic parasite or germ that multiplies within cells and causes viral infections and disease.

whitecoat: A harp seal pup, usually less than two weeks old, that still has a fluffy white coat. As whitecoats age, their fur turns yellowish, then gray.

Organizations to Contact

Canadian Department of Fisheries and Oceans
200 Kent St.
Ottawa, Ontario
Canada K1A 0E6
(613) 993-0999
fax: (613) 996-9055
www.ncr.dfo.ca/

This branch of the Canadian government manages all aspects of seals. They have several pages on their website dealing with seals and the seal hunt.

Canadian Sealers Association
P.O. Box 5484
St. John's, Newfoundland
Canada A1C 5W4
(709) 722-1721
fax: (709) 738-1661
www.sealers.nf.ca/

An association formed by, and representing, Canadian sealers. They work to preserve sealing as a way of life, and to foster employment in the northeastern Canadian provinces. Their website is extensive and offers various viewpoints in support of sealing.

Convention on the International Trade of Endangered Species (CITES)
CITES Secretariat
15, chemin des Anemones, CH-1219
Chatelaine-Geneva, Switzerland

(+4122) 979 9139/40
fax: (+4122) 797 3417
www.wcmc.org.uk:80/CITES/english/index.html

CITES is the international organization that regulates the worldwide trade of endangered species.

Cousteau Society
870 Greenbrier Circle, Ste. 402
Chesapeake, VA 23320
(800) 441-4395
fax: (757) 523-2747
www.cousteau.org/

Founded by the late ocean explorer Jacques Cousteau, the Cousteau Society has been instrumental in focusing worldwide attention on the need to preserve the ocean environment.

Earthtrust
25 Kaneohe Bay Dr., Ste. 205
Kailua, HI 96734
(808) 254-2866
fax: (808) 254-6409
www.earthtrust.org/

This organization helps to preserve marine mammals and their environment. Earthtrust also runs "DriftNetwork," a program that seeks to educate the public on the problems of commercial drift nets and on the need for sustainable fisheries.

Greenpeace U.S.A.
1436 U St. NW
Washington, DC 20009
(202) 462-1177
fax: (202) 462-4507
www.greenpeaceusa.org

One of the largest international conservation groups, Greenpeace is involved with most environmental problems. They have been very active all around the globe in trying to stop seal hunts, abolish drift nets, and control ocean and land pollution. There are many local offices in countries throughout the world.

International Fund for Animal Welfare (IFAW)
P.O. Box 193
Yarmouth Port, MA 02675
www.ifaw.org/

The IFAW was one of the first groups to call the public's attention to the Canadian commercial seal hunt. They have been active in persuading the Canadian government to stop commercial sealing, as well as trying to educate the public to not buy seal products.

International Marine Mammal Association (IMMA)
1474 Gordon St.
Guelph, Ontario
Canada N1L 1C8
(519) 767-1948
fax: (519) 767-0284
www.imma.org/

IMMA is a nonprofit organization dedicated to promoting the conservation of marine mammals and their habitats worldwide. They have also done several research studies on seals.

Marine Environmental Research Institute (MERI)
772 West End Ave.
New York, NY 10025
(212) 864-6285
fax: (212) 864-1470
downeast.net/nonprof/meri

MERI is an organization devoted to researching marine environmental problems. They have been active in researching the effects of pollution on marine mammals and in warning the public about the perils of continued dumping in the ocean.

National Marine Fisheries Service (NMFS)
1315 East-West Highway SSMC3
Silver Spring, MD 20910
www.nmfs.gov/

NMFS is the agency of the U.S. government that is responsible for managing marine mammals, endangered species, and marine environments and habitats. Their website is extensive and contains a great deal of information on marine mammals and their management.

New England Aquarium
Central Wharf
Boston, MA 02110
(617) 973-5222
fax: (617) 723-9705
www.neaq.org/

Considered a leader in the conservation, research, and care of marine mammals, the New England Aquarium also publishes a monthly newsletter, *WhaleNet,* which can be accessed on their website.

Scripps Institution of Oceanography
University of California San Diego
A-033B
La Jolla, CA 92093
(619) 534-8753
www.sio.ucsd.edu

A distinguished research institute, Scripps also has an aquarium open to the public and an extensive bookstore.

Sea Shepherd Conservation Society
P.O. Box 628
Venice, CA 90294
(310) 301-7325
fax: (310) 574-3161
www.seashepherd.org/

This private organization is very active in the conservation of marine mammals and their environments.

SeaWorld
1720 South Shores Rd.
San Diego, CA 92109-7995
(619) 222-6363

(800) 23SHAMU (animal questions)
www.seaworld.org/

More than just a marine park, SeaWorld is actively involved in marine mammal conservation. In partnership with Hubbs Marine Research Institute, they have pioneered many research techniques that have been valuable in helping stranded marine mammals.

World Wildlife Fund
1250 24th St. NW
Washington, DC 20037
(202) 293-4800
www.wwf.org/

One of the oldest, and most respected, conservation groups, the WWF is actively involved in conservation efforts for all wildlife, in every part of the globe.

Suggestions for Further Reading

Diane Ackerman, *Monk Seal Hideaway.* New York: Crown, 1995. Although written for slightly younger readers, the beautiful prose and gorgeous photographs make it a book for all ages.

Diane Ackerman, *The Rarest of the Rare.* New York: Random House, 1995. A book of essays, all dealing with endangered species. Written by a wonderful natural history writer, it's a fascinating and compelling book.

Rachel Carson, *Silent Spring.* Boston: Houghton Mifflin, 1962. A groundbreaking book about the far-reaching effects of toxins in our environment. *Silent Spring* caused the U.S. government to completely revise its policies on industrial toxins.

Jacques Cousteau, *The Ocean World.* New York: H.N. Abrams, 1979, 1993. A comprehensive and beautifully photographed book dealing with the many aspects of our global marine environment.

Berlie Doherty, *Daughter of the Sea.* New York: Dk, 1997. Not a factual book about seals, but rather a powerful novel that blends many Selkie, or man/seal, legends into a gripping story.

Robert Hunter, *Warriors of the Rainbow.* New York: Holt Rinehart, 1979. Written by the first president of the environmental organization Greenpeace, *Warriors* tells about the group's first years.

Sebastian Junger, *The Perfect Storm.* New York: W. W. Norton, 1997. A riveting, modern-day tale of life on a commercial fishing boat in the North Atlantic and its fate.

Farley Mowat, *Sea of Slaughter.* Plattsburgh, NY: McClelland & Stewart, 1984. One of Canada's greatest nature writers, Mowat tells of humans' arrival in the North Atlantic and the consequences to the environment. Written by a wonderful storyteller, any of Mowat's books (*Never Cry Wolf, A Whale for the Killing,* etc.) offer great reading.

David Quammen, *The Song of the Dodo.* New York: Scribner, 1996. A complex, interesting book about extinction, as shown through island ecosystems.

Works Consulted

Books

Diane Ackerman, *The Moon by Whale Light.* New York: Random House, 1991.

Caroline Arnold, *Sea Lion.* New York: Morrow Junior, 1994.

Colleen Stanley Bare, *Sea Lions.* New York: Dodd, Mead, 1986.

Annette Barkhausen and Franz Geiser, *Seals.* Milwaukee: Gareth Stevens, 1992.

Henry Beston, *The Outermost House.* New York: Penguin, 1928.

Michael Bright, *Project Wildlife: Seals.* New York: Gloucester Press, 1990.

Fred Bruemmer and Brian Davies, *Seasons of the Seal.* Buffalo, NY: Firefly Books, 1997.

Olga Cossi, *Harp Seals.* Minneapolis: Carolrhoda, 1991.

Jacques-Yves Cousteau and Philippe Diole, *Diving Companions: Sea Lion–Elephant Seal–Walrus.* Garden City, NY: Doubleday, 1974.

Phyllis Roberts Evans, *The Sea World Book of Seals and Sea Lions.* San Diego: Harcourt Brace Jovanovich, 1986.

Eric S. Grace, *Sierra Club Wildlife Library: Seals.* San Francisco: Sierra Club, 1991.

Sylvia A. Johnson, *Elephant Seals.* Minneapolis: Lerner, 1989.

Vassili Papastavrou, *Wildlife at Risk: Seals and Sea Lions.* New York: Bookwright Press, 1992.

Dorothy Hinshaw Patent, *Seals, Sea Lions, and Walruses.* New York: Holiday House, 1990.

Randall R. Reeves, Brent S. Stewart, and Stephen Leatherwood, *The Sierra Club Handbook of Seals and Sirenians.* San Francisco: Sierra Club, 1992.

Jack Denton Scott and Ozzie Sweet, *The Fur Seals of Pribilof.* New York: G. P. Putnam's Sons, 1983.

Lynn M. Stone, *Elephants from the Sea: The Northern Elephant Seal.* Vero Beach, FL: Rourke Corporation, 1991.

John Bonnett Wexo, *Seals, Sea Lions, and Walruses.* Mankato, MN: Creative Education, 1987.

Newspapers

Eric Niller, "Will Saving a Few Marine Mammals Put the Rest at Risk?" *San Diego Union-Tribune,* February 25, 1998.

Don Terry, "Battered Sea Lions Find Refuge from El Niño," *New York Times,* February 16, 1998.

World Wide Web

Donald M. Anderson, Biology Department, Woods Hole Oceanographic Institution, "More Monk Seal Info," www.maritimes.dfo.ca/science/mesd/he/lists/phycotoxins/msg00014.html.

Marc Bretzfelder, "Artificial Reproduction: A Last Hope for Some Endangered Species," Smithsonian News Service,

February 1989, www.si.edu/natzoo/zooview/newsserv/artrepro.htm.

Canadian Department of Fisheries and Oceans website, www.ncr.dfo.ca/.

"Canadian 1997 Seal Hunt Kill Totals In: More Than 250,000 Seals Reported Killed," Sea Shepherd Conservation Society, www.seashepherd.org/se/seca97.html.

Canadian Sealers Association website, www.sealers.nf.ca/.

"The Caribbean Monk Seal (*Monachus tropicalis*): Extinct," Endangered Species Classroom, Out of the Classroom . . . Into the Wild, www.ckmc.com/bagheera/clasroom/casestud/carbmonk.htm.

Andrew Christie, "The Tragic Return to Commercial Sealing," Sea Shepherd Conservation Society, www.seashepherd.org/se/setback.html.

CITES website, www.wcmc.org.uk:80/CITES/english/index.html.

"CITES: IFAW CITES," www.ifaw.org/cites.htm.

Tim W. Clark and Richard L. Wallace (Yale University), "Understanding the Human Factor in Endangered Species Recovery: An Introduction to Human Social Process," University of Michigan Endangered Species Update, www.umich.edu/~esupdate/library/98.01-02/clark.html.

Merritt Clifton, "Sealing Their Doom," reprinted from *Animal People,* envirolink.org/arrs/news/sealing_doom.html.

"Clubbing 'Cruelty' on Camera," BBC News Online: World: Americas, news.bbc.co.uk/low/english/world/americas/newsid_79000/79005.stm.

Peter Dyrynda and Rob Symberlist, "Sea Empress Oil Spill: Marine Mammals," University of Wales Swansea School of

Biological Sciences, www.swan.ac.uk/biosci/empress/mammals/mammals.htm.

"Depleted Species," U.S. Dept. of Commerce, National Oceanic and Atmospheric Administration, NOAA Fisheries, kingfish.ssp.nmfs.gov.prot_res/mammals/depleted.html.

"Earthtrust's 'DriftNetwork' Program," Earthtrust, www.earthtrust.org/dnw.html.

"Ecological Interactions: The Facts About Seals and Cod in the Northwest Atlantic," International Marine Mammal Association, www.imma.org/ecoconf.html.

"Endangered Species Update," University of Michigan, www.umich.edu/~esupdate.

"'Filthy Fifty' Top Pollution Licenses Identified by Greenpeace," Greenpeace press release, www.greenpeace.org/home/ffp/pub/campaigns/cdromgp/toxics/prt883.

"Final Conservation Plan for the Pribilof Islands Northern Fur Seal," *North Pacific Fur Seal,* National Marine Fisheries Service, 1993, www.nmfs.gov/tmcintyr/depleted/furseal.html.

"Gill Nets," *UWC Enviro Facts,* University of Western Cape, South Africa, www.botany.uwc.ac.za/EnvFacts/gill/index.htm.

"The Growing Seal Population in the Gulf of Maine," Fact Sheet 3, New England Aquarium, whale.wheelock.edu/whalenet-stuff/seal_factsheet3.html.

Dr. Frances Gulland, "Environmental Sentinels: The Canary in the Coal Mine," from an address to the American Veterinary Medical Association, www.tmmc.org/canaries.htm.

"Harbor Seals, XI. Conservation," SeaWorld Busch Gardens, www.seaworld.org/HarborSeal/hsconservation.html.

"Harp Seals: Fragile Victory," Greenpeace Wildlife, www.greenpeace.org/home/gopher/campaigns/oceans/pre1991/hrpsls.txt.

"Hawaiian Monk Seal," U.S. Dept. of Commerce, National Oceanic and Atmospheric Administration, NOAA Fisheries, kingfish.ssp.nmfs.gov/prot_res/pinniped/hawaiian.html.

Janet Herrlinger and Peter Erdman, "The Baby Seal Trade," gurukul.ucc.american.edu/ted/BABYSEAL.htm.

Lynda Hurst, "Experts Question Slaughter of Seals," *Vancouver Sun,* February 2, 1996, envirolink.org/arrs/news/experts_oppose.html.

International Marine Mammal Association website, www.imma.org/imma.html.

"Introduction" (drift nets), Earthtrust, www.earthtrust.org/dnpaper/intro.html.

David Lavigne, "The Sudden Ecologists," *BBC Wildlife,* vol. 14, no. 1, January 1996, p. 57. www.imma.org/sudden.html.

"Marine Mammal Protection Act of 1972," U.S. Dept. of Commerce, National Oceanic and Atmospheric Administration, NOAA Fisheries, kingfish.ssp.nmfs.gov.prot_res/mmpahome.html.

"Market for Seal Penises Prompting Unregulated Hunting of Protected Species," SeaWeb Ocean Update, April 1998, from S. Malik et al., "Pinniped Penises in Trade: A Molecular-Genetic Investigation," *Conservation Biology,* vol. 11, no. 6, pp. 1365–1374, www.seaweb.org/16update/seal.html.

"Mediterranean Monk Seal," Mediterranean Monk Seal Home Page, Phil Gibbs, November 17, 1997, www.weburbia.demon.co.uk/pg/seal.htm.

A. Kimo Morris, "The Rare Hawaiian Monk Seal," www.rviscore.org/kimo/MonkCL.html.

Doreen Moser, "Is El Niño Here? Ask a Fur Seal," The Marine Mammal Center, www.tmmc.org/shoot1.htm.

"New Seal Hunt Figure Condemned by Animal Welfare Groups," www.ifaw.org/news231g.htm.

"New Threats to Seals," www.fondationbrigittebardot.fr/uk/reprise.html.

"North Pacific Fur Seal Conservation Efforts," U.S. Dept. of Commerce, National Oceanic and Atmospheric Administration, NOAA Fisheries, kingfish.ssp.nmfs.gov.prot_res/depleted/frsealre.html.

"NRaD Technical Document 627, Revision C, Annotated Bibliography of Publications from the U.S. Navy's Marine Mammal Program, Update February 1992," www.rtis.com/nat/user/elsberry/marspec/navybib.html.

"Pinnipeds: Seals and Sea Lions," U.S. Dept. of Commerce, National Oceanic and Atmospheric Administration, NOAA Fisheries, kingfish.ssp.nmfs.gov.prot_res/pinniped/pinniped.html.

"Research: Marine Environmental Research Institute Chronology of Marine Mammal Die-offs with Selected References," Marine Environmental Research Institute, downeast.net/nonprof/meri/res.html.

Shannon Ross and Matt Hageman, "Salmon Fishing in the Pacific Northwest," wwwshs1.bham.wednet.edu/zodiac/hagross.htm.

Scripps Institution of Oceanography website, www.sio.ucsd.edu/.

"Sea Lions to Track Whales," from *High North News,* no. 11, November 1996, High North Alliance, www.highnorth.no/se-li-to.htm.

"Sea Shepherd Seal Campaigns," Sea Shepherd Conservation Society, www.seashepherd.org/actions/acseal. html.

Ginger Smith, "Water Pollution," University of West Florida, December 8, 1995, science.cc.uwf.edu/sh/curr/waterpollution/water.htm.

U.S. Dept. of Commerce, National Oceanic and Atmospheric Administration, NOAA Fisheries website, www.nmfs.gov/.

Danny Westneat, "Greenpeace Seeks Ban on Trawlers," *Seattle Times,* August 15, 1996, www.seattletimes.com/extra/browse/html/altboat_081596.html.

"Woody," Alaska SeaLife Center, www.alaskasealife.org/woody.html.

Index

Picture Credits

Cover photo: © Tony Stone Images/Natalie Fobes
© 1997 Yva Momatiuk & John Eastcott/Photo Researchers, Inc., 74
Adobe Animal Life, 13
Agence France Presse/Corbis-Bettmann, 66
© B&C Alexander/Photo Researchers, Inc., 37
© Mark Burnett/Photo Researchers, Inc., 46
Corbis, 48, 50
Corbis-Bettmann, 29, 31, 40
Digital Stock, 7, 8, 12, 16, 19, 23, 73, 82
© Simon Fraser/Science Photo Library/Photo Researchers, Inc., 54
© François Gohier/Photo Researchers, Inc., 25
© Karl W. Kenyon from the National Audubon Society/Photo Researchers, Inc., 57, 58, 80
© Tom and Pat Leeson/Photo Researchers, Inc., 63
PhotoDisc, 9, 14 (both), 15, 22
© Ron Sanford/Photo Researchers, Inc., 43
© Trotignon/Jacana/Photo Researchers, Inc., 59
UPI/Corbis-Bettmann, 36, 72
U.S. Fish and Wildlife Service, 65
U.S. Fish and Wildlife Service Photo by Bruce Eilerts, 79
© Vanessa Vick/Photo Researchers, Inc., 44

About the Author

Lesley A. DuTemple is the author of many natural history books for children, covering such subjects as tigers, whales, polar bears, moose, and others. This is her first book for young adults. DuTemple lives on the edge of a canyon in Salt Lake City, Utah. With her husband and two young children, she shares their property with a family of raccoons, a resident porcupine, several flocks of quail and songbirds, two peregrine falcons, and roaming herds of deer.